CITIZENSHIP

USING THE EVIDENCE OF
THE HISTORIC ENVIRONMENT

ENGLISH HERITAGE

ABOUT THIS BOOK

The citizenship curriculum has presented teachers with a new challenge. As well as ensuring young people gain knowledge and understanding about becoming informed citizens, teachers are asked to provide opportunities for them to develop skills of enquiry, participation and responsible action. The historic environment and those working within it can engage young people with active citizenship issues in their immediate locality, nationally and in a global context.

This book and accompanying CD-ROM aims to offer ideas and practical help by explaining the different aspects of the historic environment and how it can be used to deliver aspects of the citizenship curriculum through case studies from Foundation to Key Stage 3, including ideas for pupils with special learning needs. It also contains a toolkit section that offers some ideas on how to get started on a citizenship project about your environment. The CD-ROM contains additional case studies and resources including schemes of work and activity sheets which can be adapted by those wishing to undertake a citizenship project using the historic environment.

This book and CD-ROM will also be a useful guide for those working in the historic environment who wish to develop citizenship projects.

Throughout this book there are various links to either other sections in the book or to files on the CD-ROM.

➤ This symbol, with the relevant page numbers, refers to a section within the book.

🔵 This symbol refers to folders and files on the CD-ROM.

CITIZENSHIP AND THE HISTORIC ENVIRONMENT 4-7

This section explains how you can use issues relating to the historic environment to deliver aspects of the citizenship curriculum.

HISTORIC ENVIRONMENT 8-25

This section details what constitutes the historic environment and how each category is protected.

Archaeological sites

Conservation areas

Listed buildings

Buildings at Risk

World Heritage sites

Places of worship

Battlefields and memorials

Historic parks and gardens

Regeneration areas

RESOURCES 26-37

This section highlights resources available for undertaking citizenship projects.

Historic documents outlines useful sources and where to find them.

Maps and plans suggest how you can chart an area's history and development.

Photographs and postcards help you build up an impression of a past community.

Newspapers demonstrates how they can be a useful research tool and to express opinions.

Street features helps you pinpoint those elements that give a locality its character.

External speakers and the local community gives you ideas for involving other adults.

TOOLKIT 38-51

This section gives you ideas for setting up a citizenship project, offering issues to consider and advice on how to engage pupils.

 Getting started

 Developing a scenario 1

 Developing a scenario 2

 Collecting information

 Writing and recording

CASE STUDIES 52-67

This section features a range of projects in which pupils have considered issues relating to the conservation and management of the historic environment. All lead to an awareness of how they have a role in shaping the future of their environment, and have been selected for the transferability of their teaching approaches.

 Foundation Our High Street

 Key Stage 1 Reusing old churches

 Key Stage 1 Our home zone

 Key Stage 2 Fast forward to the past

 Key Stage 2 Building a bio town

 Key Stage 3 Our past below ground

 Key Stage 3 Futuretown and beyond

 Key Stage 3 Change in Ouseburn

 Young people with learning difficulties - The Whitefriars project

 Young people with learning difficulties - The Old Orphanage

USEFUL CONTACTS 68-69

This section lists organisations with an interest in the protection of the historic environment that can add further support to a citizenship project.

FURTHER READING AND INFORMATION 70-71

This section has a list of books and other resources which give you more detailed information about using the historic environment.

USING THE CD-ROM

The CD-ROM has four directories. Three contain files that expand on the case studies featured in this book, along with a series of additional case studies not featured. They are grouped under the following sections: primary, secondary and other projects. All case studies include a project outline and a detailed scheme of work, saved in Word, to enable you to download them and adapt them to create your own project outline and scheme of work.

The fourth directory contains:

■ additional information about aspects of the historic environment

■ support information for specific case studies described in the book

■ resource sheets and activity sheets which can be adapted to your own needs

■ scans of the images used in Developing a scenario 1 & 2.

CITIZENSHIP AND THE HISTORIC ENVIRONMENT

The citizenship curriculum seeks to promote community involvement by showing how pupils can be constructively involved in the life and concerns of their neighbourhoods. It aims to prepare young people to play an active role as citizens by developing independence and responsibility; by engaging them in collaborative research; and giving them opportunities to share their own opinions and values whilst respecting those of others. It asks for pupils to be given insights into the workings of local, regional and national government including bodies such as English Heritage. The conservation of the local historic environment can address these National Curriculum requirements as well as helping pupils develop a sense of their place within the past, present and the future of their environment and community.

Pupils at one school were asked what they thought 'citizenship' was:

"*Citizenship is being aware of the things around you that are important to the community. Being an active citizen is important, and everyone in the community has a part to play.*"

We want to build a 'sense of place and purpose' in younger generations and help them to become fully informed citizens, able to make decisions for themselves about what they want their local environment to be. By engaging with the historic environment, teachers can deliver citizenship in exciting ways by looking at real issues which affect the local community. Young people can be involved in weighing evidence, listening to opinions, and making and justifying decisions. They will have an opportunity to address real issues relevant to their daily lives and participate in the voice of their community.

The towns of Marsden and Slaithwaite in the Colne Valley near Huddersfield were undergoing various building repairs and environmental enhancement work. Two local primary schools decided to investigate how the towns were changing and whether they could have any influence on their historic environment of the future.

THE HISTORIC ENVIRONMENT

The historic environment is all around us. Whether a local church, street, public park or bridge - a castle, monastery or historic house - all provide a rich resource on our doorstep. Every part of the neighbourhood in which we live is a product of our past. Different

societies, events and influences have shaped where we live and will continue to shape any future developments. If we want young people to be active citizens, to understand their environment, to feel motivated and confident to influence the future, then we need them to understand how the historic environment is relevant to their lives today.

What aspect of a neighbourhood's past gives a community its distinctiveness? How do old buildings contribute to that distinctive character? Young people can investigate the past function and history of buildings and consider how they could contribute to the future of their community. They can consider what is important and what is worth preserving. By doing so, they will begin to understand that buildings can be valued for different reasons and that a building's function can change over time in response to the changing needs of different communities. Different groups of people may have different priorities for the preservation of their environment that sometimes causes conflict, so difficult decisions have to be made. Through the involvement of rele-

vant people from the community, pupils will be able to recognise the part played by planners, local agencies and pressure groups. They will understand the reasons for change and appreciate that people have varying needs that need to be met.

By investigating real-life issues within their neighbourhood, young people can identify how decisions affecting their local environment are made. This helps them to focus and become actively involved in the life and concerns of their neighbourhood. They should feel that their opinions are valued and lead to positive action to create change.

As part of their summer term 'activity days', a group of Key Stage 3 pupils from The Marches School, Oswestry worked with English Heritage, a local conservation officer, an architect, and Shropshire Records & Research on a history and citizenship project. Over two days they investigated the question - What should happen to Oswestry's disused railway station?

Year 5 pupils from St Andrews Maghull CE Primary School in Merseyside made a comparative study of the Rope Walks regeneration area in the centre of Liverpool and the rural area around the school. They explored the homes and occupations of the residents of the Rope Walks from 1851-1891 and discussed how some of the empty buildings could be used in the future.

THE CITIZENSHIP CURRICULUM

Using the historic environment as a stimulus can address aspects of the citizenship National Curriculum knowledge, skills and understanding statements at all key stages.

Key Stages 1 & 2: Preparing to play an active role as citizens
Key Stage 3: Developing knowledge and understanding about becoming informed citizens
Pupils should be taught:
■ to research, discuss and debate topical issues, problems and events to resolve differences by looking at alternatives, making decisions and explaining choices
■ to use their imagination to consider other people's experiences and be able to think about, express and explain views that are not their own
■ what democracy is, and about the basic institutions that support it locally and nationally
■ that resources can be allocated in different ways, and that these economic choices affect individuals, communities and the sustainability of the environment.

Key Stages 1 & 2: Developing confidence and responsibility and making the most of their abilities
Key Stage 3: Developing skills of enquiry, communication, participation and responsible action
Pupils should be taught:
■ to think about topical social and cultural issues, problems and events by analysing information and its sources
■ to talk and write about their opinions, and explain their views on issues that affect themselves

and society
■ to contribute to group and class discussions, and take part in debates
■ to face new challenges positively by collecting information, looking for help, making responsible choices and taking action
■ to reflect on the process of participating.

SKILL DEVELOPMENT
Dealing with citizenship issues within the historic environment involves enquiry by asking questions, looking for answers and making decisions. Pupils can develop effective problem solving and communication skills as well as learning to work together, giving ground where necessary to ensure a reasonable outcome. Where projects involve presentations to members of the local community, pupils must not only form and communicate their own opin-

ions but must also justify their position with reasoned evidence to back it up.

Undertaking citizenship projects in the historic environment pupils should develop skills in:
■ observation
■ comparison
■ making informed judgements
■ justifiable decision-making
■ communication
■ negotiating with others
■ creative thinking
■ problem solving
■ reflection.

Curriculum time
There are three possible forms of curriculum provision for delivering citizenship, and schools can be flexible and innovative in the ways they achieve this:
■ discrete curriculum time: this separately planned curriculum time could be a whole school project which focuses on a citizenship

---

QCA Scheme of Work Key Stages 1 & 2 (Years 3-6): Unit 9 Respect for Property
As part of this unit from the QCA, children learn about their responsibility to respect other people's property by working in groups to formulate ideas and devise strategies to improve their local area by suggesting new uses for empty buildings. They are encouraged to:
■ list the things that have happened to the building since it became empty eg. broken windows, graffiti
■ devise enquiry questions about the building
■ explore what should happen to it in the future
■ use a range of sources (including photographs, newspaper cut-

tings and information from the local planning office) to record answers to their enquiry
■ examine and record any special architectural features
■ compare the building with others nearby to determine the character of the area
■ consult with members of the local community about what they think should happen to the building
■ understand the planning process
■ devise a proposal for the future of the building and present their ideas to their peers and invited guests.

www.standards.dfes.gov.uk /schemes2/ks1-2citizenship/cit09/ 09q4? view=g

issue within the local community
■ teaching within and through other subjects: local history, geographical study of your locality, realising needs of people in design and technology, art
■ special events: citizenship-themed activity days or celebrating a local community anniversary.

Making connections

The historic environment has a wide application as a resource. It can be the stimulus for what is already taught in school, such as history and geography, as well as offering new issues for in-depth coverage.

Developing citizenship within the context of the historic environment can promote social and cultural development and may provide the mechanism by which young people connect directly with their heritage. It will enable them to make links between people's actions and the shape of their local environment, and to understand why change takes place. It will inform young people's perception and vision of the future of their local historic environment and the role they might play in its future. This is active citizenship.

Mill View Primary School's Year 6 pupils designed logos for the back of car parking tickets to promote existing shops in the area round Chester Station. One was selected and Chester City Council produced thousands of tickets for two of its city centre car parks.

Pupils from Capenhurst CE Primary School were asked for their opinions on Chester Railway Station.

Appearance and cleanliness
"Chester Station is a very old building with beautiful ironwork and stone arches. However it was dirty and there was graffiti on the floor and seats because there were no bins."

Health and safety
"At Chester Station the floor is slippy so Class 3 think they should provide gripped floors, then people will not fall over."
"... provide wheelchairs for the disabled and the elderly. There should be more warnings like when you are to close to the line you could fall onto the rail track and get killed."

Access
"Luggage attendants and luggage trolleys could be helpful, when people have lots of luggage they might need help."

Information
"The train information was good and clear on the boards but there were empty leaflet boxes. These should be checked regularly and filled up."

Facilities
"Chester Station has a bad waiting room because the toilets are not open all day ... also they need to paint the whole building."

ARCHAEOLOGICAL SITES

An archaeological site is a place or area where there is evidence of past human activity. Many are fragile and easily damaged or destroyed by modern activities such as development, agriculture, pollution, rain, and even by unmanaged tourism. Some archaeological sites have been known about for centuries, but many more are recognised by archaeologists using a number of methods, such as aerial photography. However, a large number are only discovered when development, such as road construction or new building, is proposed on a site previously undeveloped or occupied.

PROTECTION OF ARCHAEOLOGICAL SITES

The issues which determine whether an archaeological site is protected from activities that may damage or destroy all or part of it are complex. A number of factors are involved, including the type of activity or development proposed, and the local and national importance of the archaeological remains.

1990 Archaeology and Planning Guidelines

In 1990 the Department of the Environment issued guidance for planning and archaeology so that development plans should include policies for the protection, enhancement and preservation of sites of archaeological interest and their settings. This guidance stresses the importance of early consultations between developers and planning authorities to determine the likely existence and importance of archaeological remains on a site of proposed development. If the site is archaeologically sensitive, the authority may ask the developer to arrange for an assessment to be carried out by professional archaeologists and, if necessary, recommend that an archaeological field evaluation, such as a trial trench, be carried out. Once the authority has sufficient information to assess the importance of the archaeological remains, the planning decision can proceed. If the archaeological site is of sufficient importance, the developers may be instructed to alter the plans to minimise the impact on the site or, if preservation in situ is not feasible, to provide for archaeological excavation before any development can take place and to preserve the site by recording it. In some cases planning permission may be refused.

Scheduled Ancient Monuments

These are monuments considered to be of sufficient national importance to be given legal protection. A monument can be added to the list of scheduled sites by the Secretary of State for the Department of Culture, Media and Sport (DCMS), whose consent must be sought before any works can be carried out which may affect it. Scheduled monuments range from the earliest prehistoric occupation sites to twentieth-century industrial sites and defences. They include buildings (usually disused as those still in use tend to be listed), ruins, earthworks and archaeological remains.

Currently there are over 18,300 scheduled monuments (about 31,400 actual sites).

Sites and Monuments Records

Sites and Monuments Records (SMRs) are computerised records of all archaeological finds and every known archaeological site and historic building. Each find or site has an individual record containing known information such as exact location, ownership and what is known about the site. SMRs are maintained by archaeologists, often in local authority planning departments, museum departments or with the local archaeological units. They were developed mainly for planning purposes and for the control of development.

> Contacts pages 68-69
> Newspapers pages 32-33.

Corbridge Roman Site.

CASE STUDY

SAVING OUR HERITAGE

The preservation of ancient monuments can sometimes be at the centre of a local debate and can offer pupils a real-life issue to research and discuss as part of citizenship. Why do we want to conserve the past? Who benefits? What are your opinions?

Role play or debating techniques can be used so pupils begin to understand how a community can be involved in an issue, and they can begin to recognise the part played by planners, local agencies and pressure groups. Pupils can express their own views and can learn to make well-informed suggestions for the future.

SAVING GROUNDWELL RIDGE
In 1996, whilst working on a large housing development, some workmen near Swindon came across a stretch of ancient wall. Following a geophysical survey, it was thought to be a Roman villa. For the next eighteen months this important site was under threat as money was not available to buy the land from the developers. A local campaign to save the site got underway and in 1999 the Secretary of State for Culture, Media & Sport agreed funding to be released to purchase the site

and designated it a scheduled ancient monument. In 2003 various archaeological digs have confirmed that it is more likely a large Roman working farm.

As part of their history work on the Romans, a primary school studied what was happening at Groundwell Ridge. The controversial issues surrounding the site allowed the teacher to include aspects of citizenship into the work. Before visiting the archaeological dig, she looked at the work of archaeologists.

During their visit to the dig, pupils looked at the work of the archaeologists, the reasons for the villa's location and what clues indicated its possible status and importance. They also investigated the area surrounding the site, including the new housing development, by evaluating what they liked or disliked about the setting. The teacher began a discussion on - 'Should modern developments have precedence over the past?' 'Should ancient sites be freely open for people to visit?'

Back in school, the pupils looked at a selection of articles and letters in the local newspaper. They used this information plus the work they did on site, to identify the different groups of people involved in Groundwell Ridge, for example English Heritage, Swindon Borough Council, the developers, local residents and the readers of the local newspaper. A role play debate was undertaken discussing the question - 'Should Groundwell Ridge be saved?' - with pupils representing different points of view. A vote was taken at the end to show the pupils' opinion on the future of this monument. Their work was exhibited in the school hall, and parents and other pupils were invited to view it.

↖ Case Study - Groundwell Ridge
↖ Resources & Information Sheets - newspaper articles, artist's impression

---

An archaeological reconstruction showing how the Roman buildings at Groundwell Ridge may have looked.

CONSERVATION AREAS

The streets and buildings of our villages and towns are part of the historic character of our country. Their pattern of growth has created a local identity, generating the distinctive townscapes we see today.

WHAT IS A CONSERVATION AREA?

A conservation area is a defined area designated for its special architectural or historic interest, whose character or appearance is worth preserving or enhancing. First established in 1967, conservation areas have grown steadily in number. Currently there are over 9,000 in England. Local authorities have a duty to designate these

areas and use them in their planning policies to protect the character of towns and villages.

Many features within a conservation area contribute to its special character. People who live within them may have to obtain permission before making changes to a building or the area. This ensures that any alterations do not detract from the area's appearance.

> Regeneration pages 24-25

Government grant schemes

Grants may be available to enhance and improve the historic environment of conservation areas. Any development must be suitable to the character and appearance of such areas. More recently, grants have been given for the regeneration of conservation areas suffering from the loss of a key industry such as mining, fishing or agriculture. Often these schemes are administered by English Heritage and implemented by a local authority. They aim to promote the repair and enhancement of historic buildings, allowing them to play a role in the social and economic regeneration of villages, towns and cities so creating safe and sustainable communities. The schemes concentrate on employment-generating activities that form the focus for community life and prosperity, and through the repair of buildings encourage continued local employment, provide new homes and encourage inward investment. Details about current grant schemes can be found on the English Heritage website (see Further Reading and Information pages 70-71).

↖ Case Studies - Liverpool Rope Walks, Dover, Whitefriars, Our High Street,
> Change in Ouseburn
> Listed Buildings pages 12-13

CASE STUDY

THE FUTURE OF OUR AREA

What aspects of a town's past give the community and locality its distinctiveness? Looking at issues which affect the local community can support the study of citizenship and give young people an opportunity to understand how a locality has developed, and allow them to formulate and express their own opinions on what they would like their locality to be like in the future.

LIVERPOOL ROPE WALKS

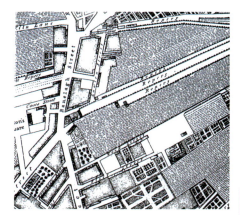

The area known as the Rope Walks in Liverpool.

The Rope Walks is named after the rope makers and maritime industries that grew up there in the sixteenth and seventeenth centuries to provide for Liverpool's shipping trade. As the port developed, it became a fashionable area for merchants, who stored their goods in warehouses either attached to or close by their homes. More recently, the area has declined as maritime activity moved away. Land became cheap and developers seized on this opportunity for cheap redevelopment projects. The area is a conservation area with over ninety listed buildings.

This project allowed pupils to study the history of their locality whilst introducing them to the democratic processes that influence conservation and the development of their own historic environment.

Pupils were asked to consider what it is about the Rope Walks area that makes it distinctive, and how old buildings contribute to this distinctive character. Pupils were told that Liverpool City Council has limited resources and wants them to advise on which of six buildings should be saved. In groups, the pupils discussed and then prioritised photographs of the six buildings in a pyramid shape with the most important on the top. Each photograph had a caption giving basic information about the building shown. After looking at each group's choice, they discussed why buildings are important and they identified what needs a local community would have of an area where it lives and works, for example facilities, housing, education, shops, open spaces. This was extended to consider how these needs differ for different groups of people like the elderly or young children. A survey was undertaken to gauge the views of peers, parents and grandparents.

Each group visited the six buildings in the Rope Walks and recorded their surroundings and location. They looked at what the building was being used for today, and what they liked and disliked about it.

Back at school, the pupils summarised what they knew about each building and the historic importance of the Rope Walks, before considering how their building could be used today to meet the needs of the local community. They presented their ideas to their peers and commented on each other's proposals.

By considering the future of the Rope Walks, Year 5 and 6 pupils developed skills in comparison as well as how to make judgements and how to exercise justifiable decision-making.

LISTED BUILDINGS

Listed buildings are historic buildings that are thought worthy of protection on grounds of special architectural or historic interest. They are catalogued on a list. The definition for listed buildings is broader than for scheduled monuments and so there are far more listed buildings, currently about 440,000. The term actually applies to anything that has been constructed, so lamp posts (including those outside No. 10 Downing Street), garden walls, sundials, bridges, bandstands, canal locks, post boxes and even some tombstones are included. Many listed buildings are in current use and the majority are private houses.

HISTORICAL BACKGROUND

Although there were Ancient Monuments Acts in 1882 and 1913, it was not until 1932 that the first Building Preservation Orders were introduced so that local authorities could protect threatened historic buildings. However, very little was done until the widespread destruction of buildings by bombing in the Second World War and in 1941 the National Buildings Record was set up to compile records of war-damaged buildings. In the same year the Ministry of Works undertook regional surveys to draw up the first lists of buildings of architectural and historical importance. In 1944 the Town and Country Planning Act brought the responsibility for historic buildings under the new Town and Country Planning Ministry and although many buildings were listed, there was little protection to threatened buildings. It was not until the 1960s when new legislation put the responsibility on the owner of the listed building to obtain written consent from the local planning authority for any works that would alter the character of the building.

There are three categories of listed buildings:

Grade 1 are defined as of 'exceptional interest', and account for about 2% of buildings that are listed.

Grade 1 - the Penguin Pool at London Zoo, designed by Lubetkin in 1933-34, uses reinforced concrete.

Grade 2★ are defined as being of particular importance and account for about 4% of buildings that are listed.

Grade 2 are defined as being of 'special interest' and account for over 94% of listed buildings.

Grade 2 - Cromwell Place, St Ives in Cambridgeshire.

Matters related to alterations or changes to all grades of listed building are dealt with by local planning authorities who are obliged to consult with English Heritage regional offices on cases affecting Grade 1 and 2★ buildings.

Criteria for listing

All buildings built before 1700, which survive in anything like their original condition are listed as well as most buildings dating between 1700 to 1840. After 1840 only buildings of definite quality and character are included. Special value is placed on buildings illustrating social and economic history or technical innovation. A building may be associated with a well-known person or event or it may be part of a group, for example a town square or model villages.

Grade 2★ - originally built in the inter-war years, this factory was built to give Hoover a glamorous modern image representing a Hollywood palace set in a garden. Today it is used as a supermarket.

CASE STUDY   REUSING OLD BUILDINGS

The preservation of buildings raises complex issues and questions that pupils can research and debate as part of citizenship. Sometimes listed buildings are in the centre of topical local issues. Appreciating why buildings need to be protected will help pupils recognise what is significant about their past. By looking at measures for protecting them, pupils will be introduced to democratic processes that empower them to influence any change to their environment.

THE CUSTOMS HOUSE, SOUTH SHIELDS

The aim of this project was to enable Year 7 pupils to understand the planning process and how it empowers people to be responsible for changes to their environment. In English it created a reason for pupils to write for different purposes - in this case what to do with an important local building that had fallen into disrepair. It involved letter writing, note-taking, drafting formal proposals, explanatory labelling, advertising and information-giving.

Whilst visiting the Customs House, pupils used cameras and structured activity sheets to record interesting architectural aspects, and they compiled a list of descriptive words of what they could feel, see, hear and smell. This helped them get a feel for the building and was later used to create poems.

Back at school, having looked at the letters page in a local newspaper, pupils wrote their own letters appealing to readers for personal accounts and information about the building. Then, working in pairs they designed a leaflet to highlight the importance of the building, its current condition and prompting the reader to consider ideas for a new use for it.

When considering how they think the building should be used, a planning proposal sheet was used to help pupils structure their thoughts. Having decided on a possible future use, pupils created a labelled artist's impression to show how their building would look, and wrote a formal proposal for the building's conversion. These were submitted for 'planning consent' to a class 'planning committee' of elected individuals.

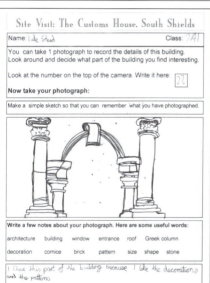

Pupils' sketches of interesting external features.

➤ Regeneration pages 24-25, Newspapers pages 32-33 Further Reading and Information pages 70-71

⬎ Case Studies - New Uses for Empty Buildings, The Old Orphanage, The Old Fire Station, Manchester's 'Water Palace', Our High Street, Chester Railway Station;

⬎ Resources & Information Sheets - planning forms

The Customs House, South Shields. In 1980 this Grade 2 listed building was in a poor state of repair. ALMA, a local group of arts enthusiasts, bought the building for £1. They raised £400,000 to convert it into a theatre, cinema and art gallery.

BUILDINGS AT RISK

All buildings are constructed to fulfil a specific function. Through time some of them are no longer needed and remain empty until a new occupier or use can be found or they are demolished. Reasons why buildings become redundant include:

■ the occupant has relocated to newer, larger more comfortable or cost effective premises

■ new technology might have superseded older manufacturing processes

■ there is no longer a demand for a particular service or product

■ a disaster occurs such as a fire.

The options for dealing with these buildings are preserving them in the state in which they are found; recycling or adapting them for new uses; restoring them to their original state using traditional or modern techniques; substantial rebuilding; or demolishing them. Many of England's listed buildings are redundant and are at risk through neglect or decay. One in twenty seven of all Grade 1 and Grade 2★ listed buildings is under such a threat.

> Listed Buildings pages 12-13

Buildings at Risk Register

The Buildings at Risk Register lists all Grade 1 and 2★ listed buildings, and scheduled ancient monuments (structures rather than earthworks) known by English Heritage to be at risk through neglect and decay, or vulnerable to becoming so. In addition, Grade 2 listed buildings at risk are included for London.

Risk is assessed on the basis of condition and, where applicable, occupancy. Assessing vulnerability

Liberty Cinema in Southall, Ealing - a Grade 2★ building at risk whose interior was badly damaged by fire. It is the only known example of a cinema built in the Chinese style. It has now been restored and returned to cinema use.

involves judgement and discretion. The condition is graded as:

■ **very bad:** a building with structural failure or instability. Often most of the roof is missing, leading to the major deterioration of the interior

■ **poor:** a building with a leaking roof, deteriorating masonry and no rainwater guttering which leads to rot and general decay throughout the building

■ **fair:** a building that is structurally sound but needs minor repairs or general maintenance

■ **good:** a building that is structurally sound and weather tight with no significant repairs needed.

The Register aims to keep attention focused on neglected historic buildings and monuments. It is used to prioritise action by English Heritage, local authorities, building preservation trusts, funding bodies and everyone who can play a part in protecting these vulnerable buildings. Priority is given to those buildings that are rapidly deteriorating and each entry is given a priority category for action from "A" for immediate risk of further rapid deterioration with no solution agreed, to "F" where a repair scheme is in progress with a user and function identified and agreed. The Register is published

annually and entries are reassessed, some removed from the list and others added.

English Heritage's role is to provide advice and resources to help owners and local authorities to secure the future of those buildings on the Register.

Use the 'At Risk' form and fact sheet on the CD-ROM to assess a local derelict building for its 'at risk' potential. Is the building important enough to be on the Buildings At Risk Register? Search the Buildings At Risk Register on the English Heritage website for any buildings in your area.

✎ Resources & Information Sheets - 'At Risk' form and fact sheet

CASE STUDY

AT RISK OF RUIN

A community's young people can become attached to individual buildings. While they grow up they see changes taking place around them. By focusing on individual buildings at risk young people can become more aware of their environment and heritage, preconceptions can be challenged, and community values shared and developed.

MANCHESTER'S 'WATER PALACE'

The Victoria Baths in Manchester is a particularly fine example of the type of public facility provided by councils during the late nineteenth and early twentieth centuries. Local people used the Baths for many years. However, by the 1990s it was in poor condition and was closed by the council. A group of enthusiasts established a trust to campaign to save this Grade 2★ listed building which is classed as a Grade C building at risk.

A local primary school embarked on a citizenship project that aimed to make its pupils more conscious of the importance of buildings to older people. The Trustees of the Baths and other local people shared their memories with the pupils, who were tasked with producing their own guide to the building to share with family and friends.

During a visit to the Baths, pupils worked in five groups, each looking at a different aspect of the building and its history. One group gathered evidence of the patterns visible on the inside and outside of the building. Their findings were to help illustrate the guide. Another group used archive material plus observation to compare the Baths, past and present. Their findings were recorded in note form, through group discussion and on tape. They interviewed Trustees and other local

Historic sports venues can be used for cross-curricular work and support citizenship as they can build upon the interests of both boys and girls.

people who had used the Baths. The third group looked for evidence of how the building had decayed since its closure. They focused upon what had lasted and what would need to be repaired before the building could re-open to the public. Group four examined the different areas of the building to note the range of activities enjoyed by visitors to the Baths. They visited the slipper baths, aerotone and Turkish baths. Finally, the last group concentrated upon finding special decorative features.

Back at school, pupils shared their findings and discussed questions such as why they thought the Baths had cost twice the usual for a building of its type? Where had this extra money been spent? Did they think it was worth it? They worked together to produce their guides.

✏ Case Studies - Manchester's 'Water Palace', New Uses for Empty Buildings, The Old Orphanage, The Old Fire Station, Our High Street

WORLD HERITAGE SITES

In 1972 UNESCO (the United Nations Educational, Scientific and Cultural Organisation) adopted the Convention concerning the Protection of the World Cultural and Natural Heritage which came into force in 1975. This World Heritage Convention is concerned with the identification, protection, conservation and presentation of those parts of the world's natural and cultural heritage that are of outstanding universal value. It has been ratified by almost 150 countries.

The World Heritage List

Any member country can submit proposals for a site to be listed. The Department for Culture, Media and Sport is responsible for nominating sites in England. The devolved administrations in Wales, Scotland and the Northern Ireland Environment and Heritage Service are responsible for choosing their nominations; the Foreign and Commonwealth Office is responsible for sites in the UK's overseas territories; and the Home Office for Crown Dependencies.

The world's first iron bridge, in Ironbridge, Shropshire.

The World Heritage Committee is made up of 21 member countries, who are elected on a rota basis. Once proposals are received the World Heritage Committee then seeks the advice of ICOMOS (International Council for Monuments and Sites) for cultural sites, and IUCN (World Conservation Union) for natural sites. To be added to the list a site must:

- constitute a masterpiece of human creative genius
- have exercised considerable influence at a certain period or within a cultural area of the world
- provide exceptional evidence of a culture which is living or has disappeared
- illustrate a significant historical period
- constitute an outstanding example of a traditional way of life
- be associated with ideas or beliefs of a universal significance.

The Convention recognises that many sites are in developing countries that do not have the means to protect and maintain their sites, so the Convention is committed to assisting the less wealthy countries.

Stonehenge in Wiltshire, one of the most famous prehistoric monuments.

The Palace of Westminster in London, renowned world-wide symbol of modern democratic government.

> Further Reading & Information pages 70-71

WHO OWNS OUR HERITAGE?

World cultural heritage can provide many issues for citizenship. Who owns our heritage - a community, a region, a nation or the world? Where are the boundaries between conservation and profit? The economics of conservation vary across the world, so should wealthier nations help poorer ones to protect their heritage?

IMPACT OF TOURISTS ON THE ATHENIAN ACROPOLIS

The Athenian Acropolis houses four main buildings: the Propylae or gatehouse to the Acropolis; the Parthenon; the Erechtheion, and the Temple of Athena Nike.
 The Parthenon was built in the fifth century BC and continued to be a place of worship until it was damaged in 1687. Since then it has been a ruin. In 1801 Lord Elgin was given permission by the occupying Turkish forces to remove some of the sculptures from the building. His agents also removed parts of the frieze. These are known as the Elgin Marbles.
 The Acropolis has been exposed to natural decay for thousands of years but more recently these have been multiplied by the effects of human action:

■ atmospheric pollution from industry and domestic central heating fumes have attacked the marble
■ inappropriate restoration techniques between 1896 and 1933
■ the number of visitors was eroding the monument.

Possible citizenship issues for discussion:

Return of cultural property: The Elgin Marbles are currently housed in the British Museum and the Greek government has formally requested their return on numerous occasions. The British argument is that they were removed legally in the nineteenth century and that their return would need an Act of Parliament.

Management of tourists: Should tourists be stopped from visiting the Acropolis? Is the tourist more important than the monument? What do tourists gain from visiting a real site that they do not get from visiting a replica? Today the million or so people who visit the Acropolis walk along designated passages. They walk over with wooden steps erected to protect the original marble ones from further erosion by their feet.

Pollution control: Should Athenians be made to cut pollution levels to save the Acropolis? What are the global implications of pollution on the world's historic environment? What is our role as global citizens?
The Greek government is undertaking various measures to reduce the level of pollution in Athens. Motor vehicles have been banned from the immediate environs of the Acropolis and there are long-term plans to replace heating oil as the main fuel for central heating.

> ✎ Resources & Information Sheets - Athenian Acropolis fact sheet, Stonehenge citizenship activities, List of World Heritage Sites

The Parthenon, a temple to the goddess Athena.

PLACES OF WORSHIP

Places of worship are an important part of our historic environment. They are tangible examples of the similarities and differences in approaches to religions, and bring us face-to-face with styles of art and design from different cultures, both living and past. Because of the care and love which goes into maintaining places of worship, they take on a special atmosphere, which is a background reminder that respect, and sensitivity for other's feelings, is an important part of a visit.

 Some places of worship are of national significance. One such building is the Shah Jehan Mosque in Woking. Sailors from the Middle East and Africa founded Muslim communities in London. These communities grew through-out the nineteenth and twentieth centuries with the first mosque being built in Woking in 1898. It remained the oldest mosque in Britain until the 1960s. Nearby is Britain's first Muslim Burial Ground, built on Horsell Common in 1917. It contains a unique memorial to the soldiers who lost their lives in the two World Wars.

Inside Exeter Synagogue.

Islamic Centre, Maida Vale, London.

 Many places of worship in this country are listed and those of exceptional historical significance form 30% of all Grade 1 listed buildings. English Heritage works with all denominations and faiths to protect their buildings by making grants for essential repairs, giving advice, and getting involved in the future if the building becomes redundant.

London Buddhist Centre, Tower Hamlets.

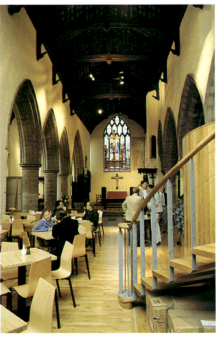

This café is free-standing and poses no risk to the fabric of this church.

Interior of Trinity Presbyterian Church in Norwich.

> Listed buildings pages 12-13, Buildings at Risk pages 14-15

REDUNDANT CHURCHES

Churches and chapels become redundant when they are no longer needed as places of worship. There are many such buildings across the country and like all empty buildings they can soon fall into disrepair. Pupils can be asked how we can protect these historic buildings no longer needed for worship. What could they be used for?

WHAT SHOULD WE DO WITH TEMPLE CHURCH?

Temple Church in Bristol is a medieval building with a leaning tower. It is under the guardianship of English Heritage. Devastated in the Blitz of 1940, it has since remained roofless but with the tower and external walls intact. This building has the potential to be turned once again into a useable building - but what sort?

Children visited the site to con-sider this question. They looked for clues to the building's past and the sort of people who would use it. They discovered round mark-ings on the ground from the earli-er circular church built by the cru-sading 'Knights of the Templar'; they considered why the tower was leaning; and they noted what dam-age was done by the bomb and what changes had taken place since 1940.

Following a discussion, the chil-dren decided that the memories and stories of local people pointed towards devising a new use for everyone, rather than a private development. They agreed that the historic features should be incor-porated into the new design, although they appreciated that cost was a significant considera-tion. The children brainstormed a range of exciting ideas.

Suggestions included a café with a crazy golf course in the former churchyard, a children's gym, a concert hall, a geology museum, a cinema and even a swimming pool!

Sketching interesting features of the building helped the children make decisions about some visual focal points for their new schemes. Everyone then mapped out his or her thoughts onto copies of the ground plan. Next, using a choice of media, each child depicted a view of their transformed building. Glass roofs, a cinema screen between a massive internal arch, and a stage where the altar had once stood, all appeared. An exhi-bition of the work toured during the autumn term to libraries, the record office, council buildings and Bristol's Architecture Centre.

> ✎ Case Studies - Temple Church, Reusing Old Churches

Contributing to the debate - children from a primary school summer play scheme in Bristol spent two days considering how this derelict church could be reused.

BATTLEFIELDS AND MEMORIALS

BATTLEFIELDS

For centuries battles have been used to settle religious, political and territorial disputes, and Britain is littered with battlefields. Some battles were part of major national conflicts; others were minor skirmishes within a local context. Some have even played a substantial part in shaping our nation and its governance. Whatever their scale, duration or magnitude, battles affected the lives of people at the time in many ways, and their outcome is reflected in how we lead our lives today.

PROTECTING OUR BATTLEFIELDS

In Scotland there is a strong tradition of protecting and interpreting battlefields such as Bannockburn and Culloden. Until recently, this was not the case in England. The threat to English battlefields came to public attention in the late 1980s when a new motorway was built which bisected the Civil War battlefield of Naseby. It highlighted that modern road building, housing, industrial and leisure developments were having a fundamental impact on these fixed points in the history of our landscape. As a result English Heritage produced the Register of Historic Battlefields.

Register of Historic Battlefields

This Register identifies 43 battlefields in England which are particularly deserving of conservation and preservation. However, the Register specifically excludes skirmishes, sieges and civil disturbances. Part of the purpose of the list is to help evaluate how the landscape has evolved around the

Site of the Battle of Flodden Field. Discuss with pupils whether they think there is any need to protect a battlefield.

battlefields. It looks at what changes have taken place since the battle and provides guidelines to influence what further development and visual impact is acceptable. Designation as a battlefield does not give it statutory protection, but is a consideration in the planning process.

> ✎ Resources & Information Sheets - Register of Historic Battlefields

MEMORIALS

Many memorials have been erected to commemorate the achievements of citizens of the past. Others commemorate significant local or national events or tragedies, which have inevitably affected the lives of a number of people. Many are permanent structures, such as tombstones, columns, statues, fountains or plaques, but some are public buildings, like schools and other educational institutions, libraries, museums and galleries, and meeting halls. Parks and gardens, too, are often named after people or events, and in them trees and seating can be found, placed there in memory of local people. Perhaps the most prolific type of memorial

is a war memorial, which can be found in almost every town and village in Britain.

War memorials

The UK National Inventory of War Memorials estimates that there are over 50,000 throughout the United Kingdom. They represent the emotional response by bereaved communities to the armed conflicts of the nineteenth and twentieth centuries. They are also a spectacular legacy of art and sculpture.

Often war memorials are taken for granted. In some cases this leads to neglect or damage through vandalism or development. The Friends of War Memorials organisation was set up in 1997 to monitor their condition and promote awareness of their historical and spiritual significance.

> ❯ Further Reading and Information pages 70-71

Statues are often used as memorials commemorating the achievements, sacrifices and contributions made by local or national figures.

Remembrance Day is a focus for many communities and brings several groups together. A visit to the local war memorial can be a key factor in developing young citizens at Key Stage One through the study of Remembrance Day.

At the village remembrance ceremony, Year 2 pupils carried a poppy wreath and laid it on the war memorial.

WHAT ARE WE REMEMBERING ON REMEMBRANCE DAY?

A war memorial was situated across the road from Forsbrook Primary School in Staffordshire, adjacent to the village church and at the centre of their community. The children walked past the memorial every day. This project aimed to use this monument to enhance children's understanding of Remembrance Day as part of the history and citizenship curriculum.

The topic was introduced with an open discussion based on the questions - 'Why do we wear poppies?' 'When do we wear poppies?' 'What are we remembering?' 'Which people are we thinking about?' 'Why is it important to remember?' They talked about the war memorial in their village and its importance in the community. There is a statue of a soldier on the memorial and the children

were interested in the details of his uniform. They were also fascinated by the list of names and recognised the names of local families.

During the week before Remembrance Sunday, the children visited the war memorial. They spent time looking, making oral observations, sketching, making notes and taking photographs. They gained a greater understanding of the significance of this monument, which they had taken for granted before.

Back in school, the children were responsible for selling poppies and they represented their school

at the local Remembrance Sunday parade in the village. On Remembrance Sunday, the Cenotaph ceremony in London was recorded, so that they could compare a national and international event with their local village ceremony. By doing this, the children joined with the wider community, taking an active part in the ceremony and the church service, which followed. The children later related their experiences to other children at school.

Case Studies - War Memorial 1, War Memorial 2

HISTORIC PARKS AND GARDENS

Britain has a long tradition of parks and gardens. From town gardens and public parks to great country estates, cemeteries and hospital gardens, all contribute to a rich and diverse landscape.

PROTECTING HISTORIC PARKS AND GARDENS

Most people know that some buildings are listed and that many ancient monuments are also recorded and protected. It is less well known that since the 1980s there has been a national record of parks and gardens which are considered to make a rich and varied contribution to our heritage, and therefore also need protection. There are 1,530 sites on the Register of Parks and Gardens of Historic Interest, which was established by and is maintained by English Heritage.

> ❯ Archaeological Sites pages 8-9, Listed Buildings pages 12-13

Register of Parks and Gardens of Special Historic Interest

This Register contains those parks and gardens considered being of special historic interest. Entries are assessed on one or more of nine criteria:
■ sites with a main phase of development before 1750
■ sites with a main phase of development laid out between 1750-1820 where much of the original landscaping survives
■ sites with a main phase of development laid out between 1820-1880 where it is important and the original landscaping survives virtually intact
■ sites with a main phase of development laid out between 1880-1939 where it is of high importance and survives intact
■ sites with a main phase of development laid out post-war but not more than 30 years ago where the work is of exceptional importance
■ sites which were influential in the development of taste
■ sites which are an early representation of a style, layout or type of site
■ sites which have an association with a significant person or historic event
■ sites with a strong group value when it is linked with buildings, land or other registered features.

There are three categories for registered parks and gardens:

Grade 1 are considered being of international significance. This constitutes 10% of the sites on the register.

Grade 2★ are considered to be of exceptional historic interest and are 30% of the sites registered.

Grade 2 The other 60% of the sites are registered as of special historic importance.

There are no statutory controls to protect parks and gardens, but local planning authorities must consider the importance of these registered sites when deciding how to deal with planning applications. They have to consult English Heritage where the application affects a Grade 1 or 2★ site, and the Garden History Society on all applications, regardless of the grade of the site.

Grade 1 - Packwood House, a sixteenth-century house, has gardens with renowned herbaceous borders and a famous collection of yews.

Grade 2★ - the Pavilion Gardens, Buxton were opened in August 1871.

Grade 2 - a cemetery in Leicester.

CHANGING OUR OPEN SPACES

Gardens are all around us. How we shape and manage them today can involve pupils in citizenship projects. For example, pupils could investigate if their local authority should design a multi-cultural garden reflecting the rich culture of their local residents.

The Water Tower Gardens

The Water Tower was built in 1322-23 to guard the entrance to the Port of Chester.

In the 1830s the surrounding land was converted into a public garden. It was changed to its present form in the late 1940s. The gardens and the surrounds are part of a conservation area, and the Tower is a scheduled ancient monument. The gardens are a community facility which is also appreciated by visitors to the city.

Year 5 and 6 pupils from St Thomas of Canterbury Blue Coat CE Junior School became involved in a SEEN project (Sustainable Environmental Education Network

- see Contacts pages 66-67). The pupils were asked for their ideas about how the gardens surrounding the Water Tower could be re-designed for creative play.

Pupils talked to officers from the City Council and learnt that some things, like the bowling greens, would stay. They also talked about the history of the site. This was followed by a visit to the Water Tower Gardens. As well as looking at all aspects of the site, they had to consider the different users: local people; tourists coming down from the City Wall; mothers and toddlers using the play equipment; older people playing bowls or just

sitting and relaxing. How could play facilities be developed which would not detract from the enjoyment of so many different people?

Working in small groups back in school, pupils began to work up their ideas then they presented their views before an invited audience which included the Lord Mayor of Chester, a local councillor, representatives of local community groups, architects and the City Council officers who would finally be responsible for delivering the scheme. Each pupil had the opportunity to speak and to be questioned by the panel.

The second stage of the project saw pupils developing creative ideas for a maze which has been installed in the Water Tower Gardens.

✎ Case Studies - Water Tower Gardens
➤ Conservation Areas
pages 10-11

REGENERATION

WHAT IS REGENERATION?

Our towns, cities and rural areas are not static, unchanging places. Over time, areas adapt and develop according to the uses they are put to and the needs of the people living and working in them. Buildings fall into disuse, or become redundant for a variety of reasons. Changes in industrial techniques and priorities, shifting population, and different employment opportunities can all contribute to decline.

Many towns and cities have interesting and sometimes beautiful groups of old buildings. Some of these may be listed for their 'special architectural or historic interest'. Some areas or groups of buildings are designated as conservation areas, as their character and appearance are considered worth preserving. However, even once-impressive historic buildings can fall into decay if positive steps are not taken to prevent this happening. Regeneration is the term given to planned and co-ordinated work on a particular area, either urban or rural, to improve its fabric, and to bring new life and economic opportunity to its community.

English Heritage is a major agency for urban and rural regeneration, working in partnership with other organisations, including local authorities, Regional Development Agencies, English Partnerships, voluntary bodies and people in local communities. English Heritage provides funding, either for individual significant buildings at risk, or for area-based regeneration.

> ➤ Conservation Areas pages 10-11, Listed Buildings pages 12-13, Buildings at Risk pages 14-15

CASE STUDY

REGENERATION AT WORK

Regeneration involves complex decisions and the setting of priorities with regard to the fate of the old and the shape of the new. These decisions present direct links to the citizenship curriculum. Often a variety of funding agencies are involved using a combination of private, public and European Community monies, so giving pupils an insight into the workings of government at many levels. Regeneration schemes can also involve the local community and pupils can gain an awareness of how community and voluntary action groups work. It can also provide them with a platform to voice their own opinions and express their ideas of what should happen to their own locality.

Changing face of Whitehaven

Whitehaven is the earliest post-medieval planned town in England and was prosperous during Georgian times. Its economy however declined towards the end of the twentieth century. In the 1990s, the Whitehaven Development Company led the restoration and regeneration of the town centre, harbour and castle. English Heritage has worked closely with Copeland Borough Council to make grants available

to owners of buildings in the area.

Four citizenship projects were undertaken by schools in Whitehaven to examine what was changing in their town.

Regeneration of Whitehaven harbour.

Regenerating the larger-scale urban landscape - the harbour: The larger-scale project is often the focal point of regeneration schemes as it has the most notable impact on the landscape, and often on the community. They are often conceived with a view to restore local pride and attract significant investment. The regeneration of Whitehaven Harbour created an area of permanent water with a marina alongside the traditional fishing facility, a museum, and renovated quays and promenades.

Key citizenship issues: What do you think about this investment in your town's future? How has the development changed the image of the town? In your opinion, is this new image good or bad?

Regenerating a streetscape - the market place: Young people are part of the community that uses the streets, so a streetscape project is particularly relevant to their interests. Whitehaven's market place is one of the commercial centres of the town, but by the 1970s it had become very run-down. A total environmental regeneration scheme was initiated - the central area was pedestrianised, key buildings were renovated, a boarded-up hotel was taken over by the local council and the streetscape was improved through the renewal of the paving.

Key citizenship issues: How successful do you think the changes to the market place have been? How can the area be improved further? What contribution can local people make? Regenerating a single building - the castle: Whitehaven Castle is seen by many as the most important building in the town. It dates back in its current form to 1769, when an older mansion was rebuilt after a fire destroyed most of its original structure. It became the town's hospital but has stood empty since 1986. The public were involved in campaigns and

Whitehaven Castle.

schemes to save the castle. With the help of English Heritage, restoration of the castle began in the 1990s and it is being refurbished by a housing association for conversion into flats.

Key citizenship issues: What use could be made of this building? Are there suitable and unsuitable uses for buildings? Should buildings be preserved at all costs? What would pupils like to see happen to decaying buildings in their town?

Regeneration on the doorstep - the bus shelter: A local youth organisation worked in partnership with Groundwork West Cumbria

on small regeneration schemes on the estates that surround the town's historic core. One such project was the improvement and decoration of a bus shelter.

Key citizenship issues: Will the young people of Whitehaven respect their environment more by being involved with its regeneration? What happens when vandalism occurs? Who is responsible for shared property?

Case Studies - Our High Street, Futuretown and Beyond, Dover, Liverpool Rope Walks, Chester Railway Station, Change in Ouseburn.

Citizenship on a small scale.

HISTORIC DOCUMENTS

FINDING HISTORIC DOCUMENTS

There is a network of historic document repositories covering the whole of Britain. These are known by a variety of names including County Record Offices, Archives, Local Studies Centres, Heritage Centres or Local History Centres. Historic documents can also be found in other places such as museums, universities and local libraries. The English Heritage archive, the National Monuments Record (NMR), has many collections of historic photographs. One large collection of these is available to visitors and indexed by parish, town and street.

Extract from Kelly's Directory of Worcestershire 1892.

Children working on a project related to the regeneration of Graingertown looked at old photographs and maps at their Local Studies Library.

The Internet has made it easier for teachers to find archive sources, as collections are being digitised and many will be accessible on line. If you want to find your nearest archive repository for local sources then you can visit the National Register of Archives web site and search by place. If you are looking for a specific source you can visit the Access to Archives (A2A) web site which allows you to search nationally by subject (see Further Reading and Information pages 70-71).

Once you have identified the most likely office, then contact them by telephone, email or post and they will be able to confirm that they have the sources you are interested in and may well be able to suggest others. They will also be able to tell you what services they can offer to teachers. Some have edu-cation officers, all should be able to offer advice and photocopies of sources, depending on condition and copyright. Owing to the unique nature of archive sources, all offices have rules about access. It is essential to make contact before taking or sending pupils in.

LOCAL STUDIES

Local studies material is generally printed and many copies would have been produced, although few of them may have survived. It also includes secondary sources, books or articles that have been written about a place or event, drawing information from various sources. Trade directories

Companies such as Kelly's pub-lished trade directories from the late eighteenth century to the middle of the twentieth century. Their main purpose was to list

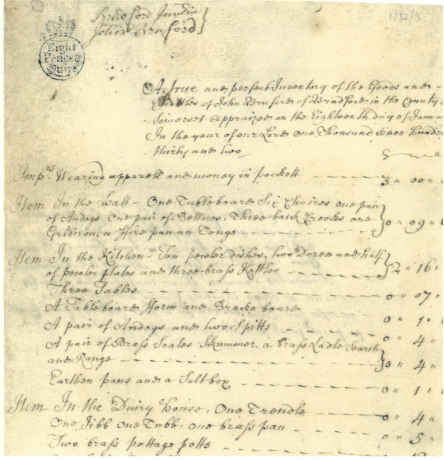

Extract of a Government Commission Report into the employment of children, young persons and women in Somersetshire.

industries and often included evidence from working people and a description of the local area. Health reports were published as a result of cholera outbreaks and included descriptions of living conditions and plans of housing.

Census

A census has been taken every ten years since 1801 (except for 1941) but information relating to individuals is not published until one hundred years have elapsed, to preserve confidentiality. The Public Record Office has the census for the whole country and is developing a website that can be used to search and order copies. Most local studies libraries and archive offices will have the 1841 to 1901 census for their own area. It will generally be on microfilm or fiche and it may be necessary to book a reader before you visit. It is usually possible to either take copies or to order them.

businesses and business people as an aid to commercial travellers who travelled from place to place to sell their goods. They also listed general information including details of postal services, transport and public institutions such as schools. Most included potted histories and descriptions of the towns and villages they covered.

Government commissions and reports

During the nineteenth century, central government began to commission and publish reports on topics such as health and employment prior to passing legislation. These were often locally based and very detailed. The employment commissions covered various

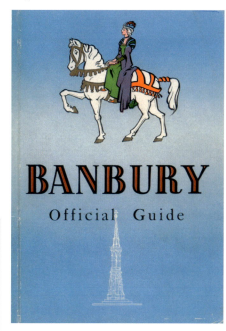

Official guides

Illustrated guides to cities, towns and large villages were popular from the 1930s and often published by the local council or a body such as the Chamber of Commerce. They were produced for residents and visitors and included information on a range of facilities including transport,

Part of the 1851 census.

housing, education, leisure and health. Some listed local industries and most contained a large number of advertisements that give a fascinating view of life in the community.

ARCHIVES

Archives are traditionally handwritten, unique documents that were produced in the course of a person's life or work, during the course of an event or by an organisation as part of its work. They will have been produced to record something as it happened and not written later as a history. Modern archive material can be in a variety of formats including film and electronic data.

Probate inventories

These exist mainly for the Tudor and Stuart periods and were room by room inventories of the possessions of a person who had died, often made by a group of their friends. They give a vivid idea of how rooms were furnished and, as many people worked as well as lived in their houses.

Church registers

Registers of christenings, marriages and burials are likely to date back to the fifteenth century for most parishes and can be used with inscriptions on gravestones to investigate families who used to live in the area. Most older registers have been deposited in record offices.

School records

Schools have had to keep extensive records since 1863 and may have even earlier ones. Not all the old records have survived, but if they have, and are not in the archives, may still be at the school. School Log Books were written up by the headteacher and recorded important events in school life. The log books sometimes give the dimensions of the school and classrooms. They also record attendance numbers, epidemics, visits of the school nurse, and celebrations of National events such as Queen Victoria's Jubilee. Pupils were not generally mentioned unless they did something out of the ordinary such as suffering an accident or passing an examination. Information about pupils was recorded in admissions registers which may also have survived.

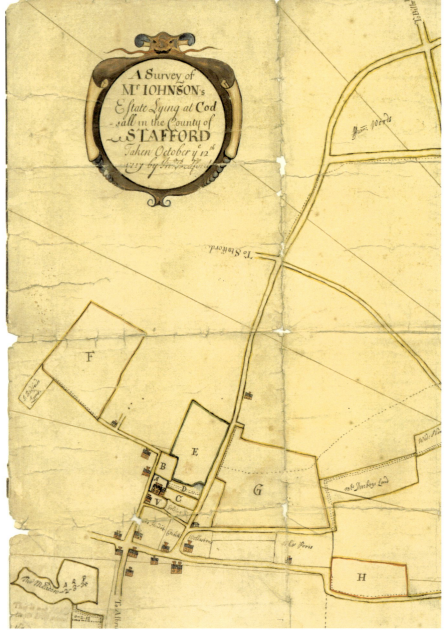

Estate agents records include files on individual buildings, old maps and plans and sale catalogues for houses and large estates.

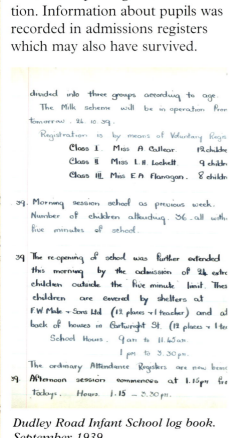

Dudley Road Infant School log book. September 1939.

MAPS AND PLANS

Historic maps are useful to uncover the story of your area as part of the research for any citizenship project. They can be used to compare a locality in the past with the present, and can show change or development over time. Historic maps are available from either a local studies library or archives office.

Printed maps

The earliest printed maps date from the sixteenth century and are generally county-based showing churches, large estates, villages and towns but no roads. Ordnance Survey maps were published for all areas in the nineteenth century. The three most useful scales for showing the development of places and buildings are the 6" to 1 mile (1:10,560); the 25" to 1 mile (1:2500), and (for urban centres only) the 10' to 1 mile (1:500). Maps at these scales were published in the second half of the nineteenth century with further editions around 1900, the 1920s, the late 1930s and the 1950s/60s for urban areas. Street maps were published from the start of the nineteenth century to accompany trade directories and are similar to a modern A-Z type of map.

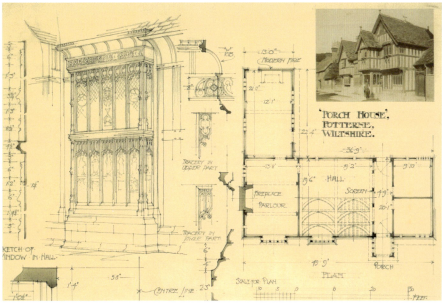

Plans will have been drawn up for large country houses, churches, schools and all public buildings and are likely to be found either in their own records or in an archives office.

Hand drawn maps

Maps were drawn of estates and adjoining fields dating mainly from the eighteenth century and will generally be found in archive collections relating to a landed family or estate agent. Enclosure maps dating from 1750 to 1850 exist for most parishes. They were drawn up to show the re-allocation of common land in a parish when the strip system of farming was changed to one based on fields. Tithe Maps were also parish based and were drawn up as a result of the Tithe Commutation Act of 1836 which replaced the tithe system for supporting the church, with a more straightforward rental charge. Please note that hand drawn maps can be very large and may not be photocopiable.

Plans

Plans drawn by an architect can be an invaluable source for studying an historic building. They may relate to the original design of a building or to subsequent alterations or extensions. Plans are also made of old buildings when they are surveyed as part of an architectural survey for bodies such as English Heritage.

Architects' plans are attractive as well as informative and you may be able to obtain photocopies although there will often be restrictions due to size or condition. Many local authority archives as well as the planning department have large collections of these plans. They can relate to individual homes or to whole housing estates. The National Monuments Record also has copies of architects' plans.

Reprints can be purchased from Ordnance Survey and via web sites including Getmapping (see Further Reading and Information pages 66-69). Your local council should be able to supply you with an up to date map at any of these scales, based around your school, although there is likely to be a charge.

PHOTOGRAPHS AND POSTCARDS

WHERE TO FIND PHOTOGRAPHS?

Local studies libraries, local history centres and archives will almost certainly have a large collection of old photographs that are indexed, most likely by street, building, area and personal names. The amount of information available about each photograph will vary. Books of old photographs can be particularly helpful, as the author will have been expected to research the images and to include as much information as possible in the caption. Most libraries and archives, including the National Monuments Record, can arrange to supply copies of photographs subject to copyright restrictions. These may be in the form of photocopies, laser copies, prints or scans.

Postcards

The first postcards appeared in 1874 and the boom time was 1902-1918. Professional photographers began to photograph their local area selling direct or supplying local publishers. Postcards which have been sent through the post have the additional attraction of stamps and intriguing messages which make images, already often a very personal and evocative source, even more so.

Collections of old photographs can give a vivid impression of an area including its community, and how it has changed. In most areas the oldest available photographs will date back to around the late 1860s.

Southernhay West Terrace, after the raids of 1942.

Windmill, Aldbourne, Wiltshire.

Women working in Crappers Cardboard Box Factory, Southwark, taken 1908.

North Road, Highgate, 1911.

Two postcard views of Bridgenorth, Shropshire. The one on the right shows the cliff railway.

Warkworth Castle and Harringay Ladder. Aerial photographs show the landscape as it really looks from the air. A single aerial photograph can answer the question: What is/was this place like? A collection of aerial photographs can answer the question: How has this place changed?

NEWSPAPERS

When your pupils are investigating a local issue, particularly one concerned with planning and development, they will need to use a variety of sources. If the topic they are investigating is in any way contentious, there will almost certainly be articles about it in the local or regional newspaper, where concerned local people can express their point of view, usually through the letters page. Sometimes the editorial team will comment on proposals, offering an opinion as well as presenting the facts, so pupils will need to be aware of this when using newspapers as a resource.

FINDING THE MATERIAL

Many local or regional newspapers will have some sort of archive or library, and although these are not always open to the public, most are happy to accommodate your research. Back copies of local and regional newspapers are usually held, often on microfilm, at main reference libraries or the county record office. Copies of articles may usually be purchased for educational use.

The majority of newspaper offices have their own photographic departments, and will sometimes release photographs no longer required for publication to schools. Larger newspapers may have a negative library, sometimes keeping the old glass plates from up to one hundred years ago. For educational projects, schools are usually able to purchase prints from these, providing the newspaper owns the copyright. If the issue, building or area you are investigating has a long history, it will be worth researching these archives. It will be important to gather as much information about the photograph at the same time, as your pupils will need its context.

USING THE MATERIAL

Pupils can use the local newspaper both as a source of information and as a vehicle for presenting their own findings or opinions. Using newspaper techniques for writing and presenting material will give your pupils practice in using different types of language. It can offer various opportunities for developing skills in literacy alongside your citizenship work.

As a preparatory exercise get your pupils to compare stories as reported by different national newspapers. Identify a story, preferably one where there will be a variety of views and versions expressed. Buy copies of different newspapers, all on the same day, and cut out/photocopy your chosen story.

Ask your pupils to compare the various accounts, looking for differences and similarities in facts, and for statements which express views or opinions. Ask them to use different coloured highlighter pens to point out variations.

Lead a class discussion. What kind of language is being used? Is it straightforward, low-key, formal? Or is it emotional, inflammatory, personal? Once differences have been explored, ask pupils to consider why accounts of the same

Newspapers as a research tool

I am Steven Hart from Redby Primary School. In school we are dong a project on the old fire station in the town. In this project we need information.
We would like to get replies from people who worked there, such as firemen, cleaners, the chief and people who lived around the station. We would like photographs, newspaper cuttings and life stories.
We would like people to send us some letters and pictures if you could.

Steven Hart, The Old Fire Station Project. Redby Primary School, Sunderland

A letter sent to a local newspaper asking for information can help younger pupils research the social history of an empty building.

event might differ. Reasons might range from the different vantage points of observers, incomplete information, different experience of previous similar events, strongly held religious or political beliefs, or because the reporter is writing for a particular purpose or audience.

Oxford Castle Prison, which closed in 1996.

OXFORD CASTLE

Oxford Castle, later Oxford Prison, lies in the heart of the City of Oxford. It is a scheduled ancient monument and many of its buildings are listed at Grade 1, 2★ and 2. It also lies in the central conservation area of the city. The Prison closed in 1996, and Oxfordshire County Council became the custodian of a unique set of buildings in an important historical setting. The Council's objectives were to:

■ secure the conservation of the historic buildings and to find sustainable new uses for them

■ provide public access to the site and as many of the buildings as possible

■ provide facilities for historical interpretation and education.

In 2000 a London-based development group proposed to take over the listed buildings and turn them into a four star luxury hotel complex, offering tourists the experience of staying in former prison cells. This scheme was granted planning permission by Oxford City Council but it was not a decision favoured by everyone.

Possible citizenship issues: What should happen to Oxford Prison? Who are the main people and organisations involved in the Prison's future? Will the people of Oxford have more access to the site of the castle and prison than previously, or not? In 2002 new plans were drawn up for the site, do you agree with what is proposed? If so, why? If not, what would you like to see happen to the Prison site?

Oxford Mail

At the heart of the community since 1928

A need for compromise

It is perfectly clear that although the city council planning committee has given its approval to the re-development of Oxford prison, there are misgivings among some councillors.

These are shared by many people outside the Town Hall.

There was always likely to be a conflict between those who wanted to protect the heritage of the site and those who saw the exciting commercial possibilities of this city-centre location. An acceptable balance had to be reached.

The Oxford Mail would not wish to see the historical significance of the site lost among a hotel, restaurants and a car park; but neither would we be happy to see the project abandoned for the sake of excessive protection of what is, when all is said and done, a man-made pile of earth.

Clearly the proposed two-storey building alongside the mound is unacceptable and the planners are to re-visit the matter. However, we would hope that opponents of the entire scheme will not persist in using this aspect of the development to sabotage the whole project. Private finance is needed to make use of what is, in the words of the planning committee chairman, a dead part of the city.

Government-sponsored agencies and voluntary groups could never hope alone to find the money needed to bring it to life.

Compromise is needed from all parties, otherwise the developers could walk away and the city would be back to square one.

STREET FEATURES

The character of a street or an area is usually defined by the buildings in them and how they are used. The buildings themselves are characterised by their different architectural features and construction materials. Many have decorative features, especially those frequently seen in residential or shopping streets, which have their origins in earlier periods of building design.

Apart from the buildings, there are many other features which contribute to the character of the area. You will see in any street in towns, cities and villages across England a wealth of objects, placed there for a variety of reasons. Mostly, these are functional, but some are purely decorative.

Use the following as a starting point for features to find on streets and buildings in your school's locality.

Look up

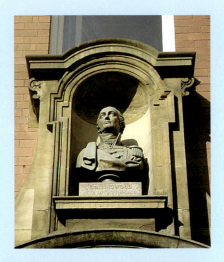

Look down

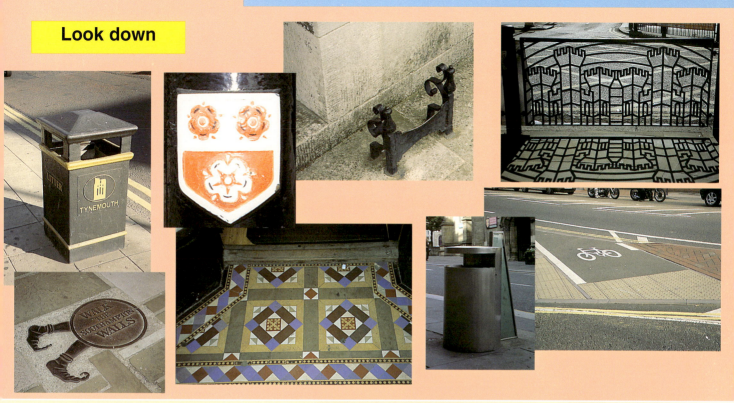

Look all around

EXTERNAL SPEAKERS AND THE LOCAL COMMUNITY

A variety of local organisations and societies can be called upon to engage young people in citizenship. Many, given adequate notice and briefing, can provide speakers. Some will be able to come to school whilst others will invite the class to visit them on site.

The advantage of using these external speakers is that they bring a fresh perspective to a project as well as introducing a new voice to pupils and providing them with an opportunity to develop their questioning technique. Through this experience, pupils gain an insight into the wider world and are given the opportunity to:

■ discuss and debate topical issues (PSHE/Citizenship)
■ talk to people in different fields about the impact of work/events
■ find out about the past from a variety of sources, for example, stories, eye-witness accounts (History)
■ fine tune their speaking and listening skills (English)
■ take part in a rich, interactive learning experience
■ have opportunities to distinguish between fact and opinion.

PREPARING THE GROUND

Some speakers will be more used to addressing pupils than others. Therefore, to get the most out of the experience and to help everyone enjoy the presentation, it is important to brief speakers. Provide information about the age and language abilities of pupils

As part of their project on the Victoria Baths, these pupils interviewed Sunny Lowry, the first woman to swim the English Channel, who told them how she used to swim at the Baths.

and their attention spans, and check the needs of the speakers themselves. They might require advice about the format of the session including:

■ recommended length of talk
■ use of audio-visual equipment
■ use of objects
■ opportunity for productive questions as often pupils only ask closed questions.

If the speaker is visiting school, pupils could draft a letter/invitation confirming arrangements. A useful activity would be for them to find a map and add their own directions to school for the visitor to follow. They could arrange a parking space if it is required.

POTENTIAL SPEAKERS

Most areas have an archaeological unit. Some are able to send a local archaeologist to talk to classes. They can give an overview of the

history of a place and explain how they have reached their conclusions. Often they bring finds such as animal bones and pottery sherds with them. The impact of these objects upon pupils cannot be over-estimated. They provide a tangible link with the past.

Council planning departments can sometimes send planners or advisers to talk about their work. From them, pupils can learn about conservation areas, listed buildings and their protection or planning developments such as new roads and the factors which have a bearing upon their construction and route. In order to consider the different viewpoints of those affected by such developments, the class would need to talk to others such as developers, architects, local residents and tourists. All the information gathered could be used to organise a debate. Or, they might make a presentation to the planning department or their parents. This work would link especially well with geography and citizenship requirements.

Other helpful contacts include archive officers and librarians. They can outline the range of sources available including census and trade directories. Sometimes they can be booked to talk to pupils about how these can be used. In addition, they can recommend local history societies or individuals. Museum education officers can provide information on strong areas of the museum's

'Experts' can be asked to come into schools or accompany groups on site visits.

collections. In many instances, they have themed collections of artefacts which they can use with pupils on site. Sometimes they can visit schools for sessions.

ENGAGING THE COMMUNITY

Nearer to home, useful contact can be made with local family firms, who having been in the area for generations, might share stories from across the decades. Other local groups like housing co-operatives or community newspaper teams can be contacted about their activities and opinions. Members of different religious communities can be invited to talk about their beliefs and practices, explaining why buildings and monuments are important to them.

WORKING WITH FAMILIES AND FRIENDS

Some of the most routinely used speakers in schools are family and older members of the community. This is especially the case where an historical event being investigated is within living memory. Pupils are able to hear stories from those who were eye-witnesses or participants. Their stories are often brought to life with the help of

their own photographs, and ephemera, for example school certificates, newspaper clippings or old toys.

It is important that pupils can distinguish between fact and opinion and are aware that some speakers find returning to school a strange and intimidating experience. They can be made to feel more comfortable in a few simple ways:

■ receiving a friendly letter from pupils explaining what they are doing and why, and including the arrangements for the day

■ being met at reception by a pupil, especially if the pupil is a member of the family

■ working with small groups of children rather than the whole class at once

■ being sent in advance one or two examples of the themes pupils are exploring

■ being offered refreshments.

If the project culminates in a special drama or event, speakers can be invited to attend as VIP guests.

These Year 12 students visited the new community centre to talk to local residents about their memories of when the Old Orphanage in Sunderland was a community centre.

Mill View Primary School communicated their findings and opinions on Chester Railway Station to decision-makers, councillors and council officers in the Town Hall.

GETTING STARTED

This chapter offer ideas on how to get started on a citizenship project about your environment, and includes some off-the-shelf exercises that will stand alone or that you may be able to adapt to real situations. It also gives advice on how to collect information using different techniques such as interviews and questionnaires.

It contains:

■ some ideas about investigating planning issues in your area

■ an imaginary example of a development issue

■ a follow-on debating exercise

an imaginary exercise on making decisions

■ advice on preparing questionnaires

■ advice on preparing personal interviews

■ advice on developing writing and recording techniques.

LOOKING AT PLANNING ISSUES

To find out what planning developments or concerns are current in your area, look at local newspapers, or, better still, contact your planning or conservation officers at your local council. Enlist their help at the beginning, not just to advise you on appropriate issues, but also on ways in which your group can investigate them, and present their findings. Planning departments seek the views of people who may be affected by their decisions, including those of young people. Presenting their work to other people who live or work in the area being looked at should also be considered from the outset.

If there is no live issue for you to investigate then turn to an area near to school, and pose lines of enquiry such as:

■ can we improve the High Street?

Young people can be given an opportunity to express their own opinions about changes that are happening around them in their historic environment.

■ how can where we live be made better?

■ can school be made friendlier and a better place to work in?

FINDING OUT WHAT THE PLACE IS LIKE

To understand the character of your area, look at its history by using old photographs, maps, trade directories or interviews with older inhabitants. Find out if there are any listed buildings or if it is a conservation area (see pages 10-11). Some sources for research are listed below.

Maps, plans and aerial photographs

These are useful in clarifying the boundaries of the area being looked at, as well as giving a bird's eye view. They show whether the place is residential or commercial, and how it is serviced by schools, shops, parks, places of worship, leisure and entertainment. KS2 and KS3 pupils can carry out land-use surveys by colour coding a map according to different uses, and quantifying the results. Is there a dominating feature, like a river, hill or prestigious building which gives the place character?

Comparing an old photograph with one taken today can show pupils what has changed.

Mark out the main transport routes - roads, rail, and pedestrian, and discuss what effect these have on the area. Combining maps with aerial photographs puts flesh on the bones of what the place looks like, giving instant information about usage and appearance of buildings and spaces. Ask pupils for immediate impressions - cramped, spacious, well-laid out or haphazard. Identify the areas of most interest and allocate, when on site, parts to groups to photograph (long views and details), to give the 'feel' of the place. Use these and the maps in a wall display to give an overview of the area.

Visual and aural records

Labelled drawings, photographs, and video can be used to record factual information. If you want drawn records of each house in a street, or each room in school, it is best to have them all roughly to the same scale. You can do this mathematically, or more loosely by suggesting that the tallest particular building or feature can be drawn to fit exactly vertically into an A4 sheet, and other buildings should be proportionate to this.

The windmill at Whitburn was built in 1786 and worked as a corn mill for 75 years. After standing derelict for one hundred years, it was restored in the 1980s and opened as a museum and interpretation centre. It is now once again empty and unused.

Personal responses can also be recorded through artwork or photography, and are good starting points for group discussions. Recording the noises and noise levels in different places is an interesting exercise, as this is an area that is usually last to be considered in planning developments, but one which affects everyone.

Physical surveys

These can be used to record both factual information and personal feelings, and show evidence of what the place looks like or how it is used. Factual information can take in:

■ building materials (brick, stone, timber, flint, concrete, glass, tile, slate, thatch)
■ traffic aids (bollards, lights, signs, road markings, crossings, cycle and bus lanes)
■ amenities (litter bins, lights, phone and post boxes, benches)
■ traffic surveys (counting the number of cars in a given time, position of bus stops, car parking usage)
■ aesthetics (sculptures, fountains, murals, building details, buskers, ephemera such as advertising billboards)
■ access (how easy is it for people with impaired mobility, vision or hearing to use the place, or for those with pushchairs).

Personal responses include:
■ likes and dislikes (green spaces, trees, birds, car fumes, narrow pavements)
■ associations (places used by drinkers or drug addicts, where fights happen, used as lavatories, where open-air concerts have taken place, used by street traders/buskers, somewhere to go for peace and privacy).

Methods of surveying can involve using headed columns (pictorially headed for KS1 pupils) in which ticks can be entered, to be added up later, or

Any students doing surveys need close supervision, and should not work in groups of less than three.

Methods of measurement can involve many techniques.

photography or video-filming (particularly good for older pupils for recording places with specific associations). Another method is to ask for the five best and worst examples of a public space, building, street furniture, spaces between buildings, or whatever is being studied. Looking at access can involve role-play using a pushchair or wheelchair, or covering eyes and ears.

Personal response

It is easy to give quick answers to what is good or bad about a place, but slowing down to consider each individual factor can be revealing. If a universal groan is the usual response to a request for creative writing, remove some of the decision-making responsibility by giving a structure, for example, ten lines, or a haiku (three lines in syllable lengths of five, seven and five), and give step by step ideas on what to do. For example, note down five things that can be seen, then add an appropriate adjective to each, and repeat the process for things that can be heard and smelt. Ask for a list of feelings about the place, and suggest that these can be described using verbs and adverbs. For example, the effect of car fumes can be expressed as slowly smothering, silently poisoning, gently killing. Introduce onomatopoeic words (sounding like the noise they depict, for example, zoom, sigh, clatter) and similes (comparing a thing to something else - the fumes are like a tidal wave) or metaphors (saying it is something else - the fumes are a tidal wave). If there is reluctance to finish the work individually, complete it as a group exercise, considering, rejecting and selecting good descriptions, but essentially sharing feelings about the area.

The Future of the Mill

What will happen to the Mill ?
A leisure centre - or better still.
There'd be a posh new door to enter.
There maybe a café for all.
Or a Disco in a big hall
Or will it be empty forever.
Imagine a huge posh house -
No place for a tiny little mouse.
A mill for making colourful cloth
Now a run down place for moths.
The future of the Mill is unknown
Can't it be turned into a luxury-home?

Other people's points of view

The starting point here is group discussions about what pupils themselves want from the high street, development area, school or the place in which they live. This can easily become a wish list, and it is important to know what other people want as well. There are various ways of doing this; questionnaires aimed at specific groups (young people, residents, workers, walkers), personal interviews, or general appeals through a newspaper. Whichever way is chosen, the important thing is to decide exactly what the questions are, and if they can be answered simply. A

Pupils can present their views in school or in a more formal 'Question Time' session with an invited panel of representatives from the various interested bodies.

good way to test for vagueness or ambiguity is to get groups to test questions on each other, and then on parents.

Debates in role

This involves providing a real or imaginary scenario and giving information about imaginary individuals with different vested interests. Working in groups, pupils take the point of view of one of the characters, pinpointing the most telling points for one of their number to argue in a debate. Give each speaker three minutes, allow questions from the floor, but then give a verdict (or better still, get someone else in from another class). There is an example of different viewpoints in this chapter, using the imaginary development exercise.

DECISION MAKING

At the end of the day, when all points of view have been considered, decisions have to be made, and they may not be satisfying to everyone. If you have not had time to embark on your own planning issue, use the example on pages 42 - 43 to get this point across.

Points for consideration include:
- effects on employment. Will a new development bring more jobs temporarily or permanently to the area? If the former, is it worth it? If permanently, are there enough existing houses or sufficient amenities?
- what are the aesthetic consequences of any alterations or new buildings? Do they fit in with the character of the area or building - are they compatible in scale, design, or building materials? Are there existing regulations (conservation area, listed building) that must be taken into account?
- will provision for traffic be increased, or will it be able to move faster? Is this a good thing for everyone? Can the existing transport infrastructure cope, or will new routes need to be made?
- will amenities, or access to them, be better? For example, will there be better shops? Will it be safer to get to school? Will the building be pleasant to work or live in?
- have the needs of all members of the community been considered? Are there any compensatory facilities for those who lose out?
- if you are looking at a communal building or a residential area, have rest and leisure facilities been considered?
- will it be a pleasing place to be? Will people want to stay or move here?
- how much will it cost? Is this realistic or proportionate? Real costs are difficult to find out, or to estimate, so it may be that all you can do is to make pupils aware that there are many demands on budgets, and the social values of projects have to be weighed against each other. An imaginary exercise on historic buildings is included in this chapter.

PRESENTATION

Presenting to an audience, whether it is another class, parents, an interested group, like a Residents' Association, or planners and councillors, gives added meaning to the work. It could take the form of an afternoon 'open day' or a formal presentation to an invited audience. Aim for a combination of display and presentations, which might include some of the following:

■ computer-generated analysis of the questionnaires and surveys

■ frieze of the street as it is and how it could be

■ a video portrait

■ a slide-tape presentation, using slides of the area with a sound commentary

■ models of the area now, and as pupils suggest it could be

■ acetates of maps of the area in the past, now, and as it might be, which can be overlaid on an overhead projector, or presented on computer

■ drama vignettes, adapted from the role play debates.

Presenting opinions and advocating change.

Campaign leaflets designed to promote public awareness of locally important buildings.

DEVELOPING A SCENARIO 1

RAILWAY END DEVELOPMENT PRESENT SITUATION

Railway End is a block of land on the outskirts of town, housing a railway warehouse, built in 1860 with no expense spared, but now empty and suffering from vandalism. Behind it is some wasteland which used to be the goods yard, and next to it are three impressive Victorian houses. These are occupied by a Post Office and general stores, a dentist, and a chemist. The upper floors are flats. There are very large gardens behind, which is where teenagers from the blocks of flats nearby go in the evenings. The surrounding area is a mixture of blocks of flats, small businesses, like the Quick Change Tyre Stop, terraced houses and Forge Lane Primary School. There are corner shops dotted everywhere, and there is a shopping centre, with a supermarket, about a mile nearer the centre of town. Running along the side of the warehouse is the railway line, and in front is East Street, which carries a lot of traffic because it is the only road crossing the railway at this side of town. There is a good bus service with stops on East Street. The town's railway station is five minutes away, but travellers needing overnight accommodation have to travel out of town to a motel.

Planning proposal

A supermarket wants to buy the whole block, demolish the present buildings and put up a new building in the company style, with car parking at the side. They say the development will add greatly to local amenities, although they hope to attract shoppers from a wide area and are providing a very large car park for them. They add that both building and running the supermarket will provide local employment.

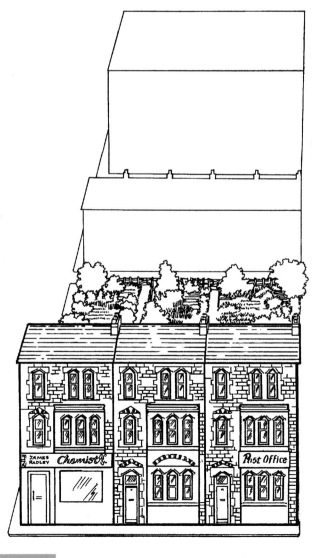

POINTS OF VIEW
Civic Trust

Members feel that the both warehouse and houses should be preserved. Both types were once common in the area, most other examples have been demolished and buildings of all styles and sizes put up their place, robbing the area of visual character and attraction, and making it depressing to live or work in. Neither sets of buildings are listed but both are good examples of solid, pleasing architecture, and could be restored to a very attractive appearance. They suggest that both sets of buildings can be converted to other uses, like offices, leisure facilities, hotel accommodation, or small businesses and workshops.

The school

The school is expanding and needs an additional playing field. It has been raising money to buy the old gardens and wasteland, but the new supermarket needs these areas.

Forge Lane Flats Residents' Association

Parents are worried that increased traffic caused by supermarket customers using the quiet back streets for access will increase the risk of accidents to schoolchildren.
The young people living in the flats are from local families and looking for job opportunities. Small children and teenagers have used the streets, wasteland and gardens as unofficial meeting places, and for football, skateboarding and rollerblading. It is unsatisfactory, but there is nowhere else to go. What they really need is somewhere safe, comfortable, and attractive.

YOUR PROBLEM

You have been asked to advise the planners. Is building a new supermarket the best development option for this area?

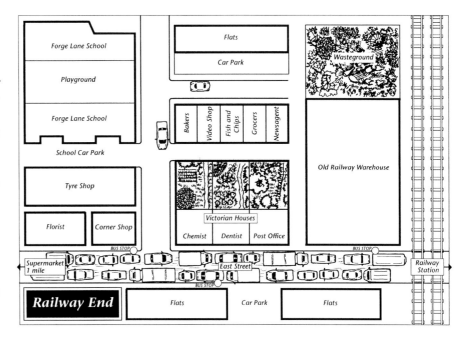

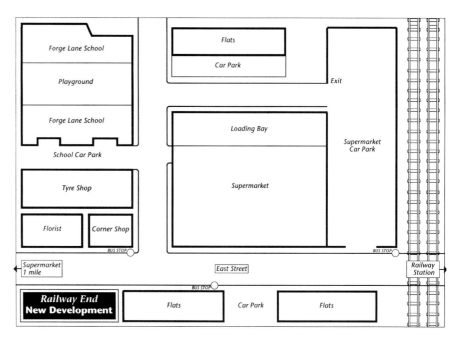

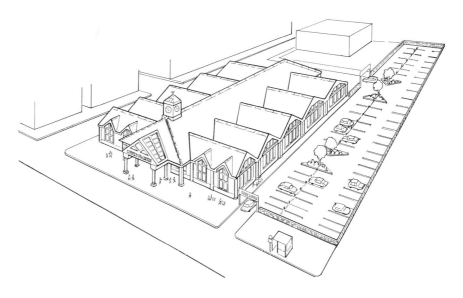

HOW WOULD YOU DECIDE?

Below are some of the people who will be affected by the Railway End development. Choose one character and use the information on the previous pages to state their point of view, and add to it if possible. If you looked at the development exercise and came up with alternative suggestions, bring these in to strengthen your arguments. Remember that you want your argument to sound the most convincing, which means that you have to understand what points other people are likely to come up with.

Mike and Tracey Flanagan, just married
I think it would be great if we get a supermarket. We want to live here near our families, but there is not much work. The supermarket gives us both the chance of jobs. Otherwise all of us young couples will have to live somewhere else, and it will be all old people round here.

Mr and Mrs Fletcher
We run the Post Office and stores. The supermarket will put us and the other small shops out of business. Many of our customers are old folk, and they cannot get to the main Post Office. It is sometimes the only time they see anyone else to talk to, and we keep an eye on them.

Karen Smith

I have a baby and a child of two. A supermarket next door means I do not have to drag myself and the pushchair onto the bus to go into town.

John Harrison

I live in one of the Victorian houses. I think it and the warehouse next door, give the area a bit of interest - most of the other buildings are just concrete blocks or rows of houses. All the same, it is a bit run down, but if it were repaired it would be a real feature round here.

Jackson Davies

I just want somewhere safe to go with my friends. If we skateboard in the street, there is always a car every so often that we have to stop for, and if we go into the gardens, there are sometimes people taking drugs there because they cannot be seen from outside.

Mrs Patel

I am a governor of Forge Lane School. The supermarket will be really bad for the school. There will be more traffic, and that pollutes the air as well as being dangerous. Also we will not be able to have our extra playing field which we really need.

DEVELOPING A SCENARIO 2

Bromfield Council has decided to create more employment in the town by improving its appeal as a tourist destination. They have identified six projects that will help Bromfield as a tourist attraction, but unfortunately their budget of £1,000,000 will not cover all the costs involved.

Decide how to spend the money: you need not allocate money to every project, or all the money each needs, but you do need to explain your decisions.

Bromfield Museum
This was originally the home of Bromfield's most famous person, an artist called Anne Claret. At present it contains glass cases of items relating to local life, donated by local people who are generally very proud and protective of the museum. The curator wants to redisplay the contents in a much more lively way, and to add a shop and café.
Cost £300,000

Canal Street Mill
Now redundant, this was one of many Victorian textile mills which characterised Bromfield, but few are now left. It is in good condition and could easily be divided into small shops or much needed workshop areas, but it would be expensive to ensure it conforms to existing health and safety and access regulations. It is not near the town centre but the canal passes down one side, and, if cleaned up and the banks made safe, it could provide an attractive setting.
Cost of renovation £500,000
Cost of tidying up the canal banks £100,000

Little Rosewood Hall

This is a timber-framed building in the heart of town, owned by the local Civic Society. It is one of the oldest buildings in town and is in urgent need of repair. At present volunteers guide people round it, but the Civic Society wants to make it into a heritage centre, showing the history of the town and its buildings. The Council wants to install a Tourist Information Centre on the ground floor.

Cost Heritage Centre £300,000
Tourist Information Centre £100,000

Bromfield Hall

This is a large manor house on the outskirts of town. A hotel chain wants to make it into a conference centre and hotel, with a tournament standard golf course, but will only do so if the Council agree to improving the road which serves it. The road will cost £500,000 and, if approved, the hotel company is prepared to spend £2,000,000 on the conversion. The golf course could put the town on the map as a sporting venue, and the hotel will bring in visitors who have money to spend, as well as providing employment.

Cost £500,000

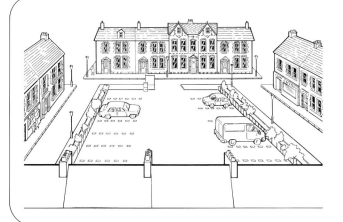

Westchurch Square

A square of family-sized Victorian houses in the centre of town, none of them historically important, but pleasant, with some made into shops. There is not much traffic, but there is a small car park in the centre. The Council want to ban cars, replace the car park with benches, trees and a fountain, and encourage coffee shops with pavement tables.

Cost £100,000

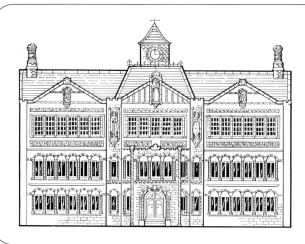

Town Hall

A very ornate, large Victorian red-brick and stone building, with stone details and statues set into niches on the frontage. The building looks run down because the stonework is badly eroded, and needs replacing or removing. Removal would seriously detract from the grandeur of the building.

Cost of repair £200,000
Cost of removal £100,000

COLLECTING INFORMATION

DEVISING QUESTIONNAIRES

Basically the questions 'Who?' 'What?' and 'How?' need to be sorted before a questionnaire can be drawn up. Who is the target audience? Is it residents, workers, other people using the same building, young people, older people, shoppers, or tourists? Whoever it is will affect the content and possibly the style of the questions.

What you need to know sounds obvious, but questions need to be specific, so it is a good idea to recap as a class what is already known and what needs to be found out. Having a very clear idea of why you want the answers helps immensely in framing the question unambiguously.

How you put together the questionnaire depends on whether you want quantifiable answers or quotable opinions. If you want answers that are easy to collate, go for questions involving yes/no answers, or for which you can provide tick boxes indicating degree (bad, acceptable, good, excellent) or preference (specific choices to tick).

Questions to which people give their own unstructured answers or opinions are hard to collate, but give a more colourful view. A combination of the two, with tick boxes and a space at the end of the question or questionnaire for a fuller response could be used.

Questions need to be neutral and not biased in order to produce a favoured answer, and should have a logical sequence, with one leading on to the next.

If the questionnaire stands alone, and is not part of a personal interview, it should have an introduction explaining what it is about,

Pupils from Queen's Park High School surveyed passengers at Chester Railway Station as part of a geography and citizenship project that aimed to provide information to assist planners with the redevelopment of the station area.

who is responsible for it, and what will happen to the answers. A decision should also be made about identification or the need for a name; how you will deal with age (use a general range rather than actual years); and do you need to know their occupation.

Different groups can be responsible for questionnaires aimed at different groups, and a good way of testing it is on parents, so that any difficulties can be ironed out before it is used in earnest.

Decide who is going to be responsible for layout and design, distribution and analysis, and if any money is available.

Distribution

Issues to consider include:
■ how the questionnaires will be distributed and collected (geographical areas, by post, by hand, personal interview)?

■ how many to distribute (not everyone will respond)?
■ how the questionnaires are actually going to be reproduced?
■ deciding on a timescale for return and analysis
■ checking the safety and supervision of pupils if any personal interviewing or distribution is taking place
■ remembering to thank people for their time.

The analysis can be compiled and presented using ICT, with results in numbers, descriptions, bar charts or pie diagrams.

Key Stage 1 pupils from Capenhurst Primary School devised a questionnaire and surveyed passengers at Chester Railway Station. They were assessing what they liked and disliked about the station.

CONDUCTING INTERVIEWS

The important things to concentrate on when preparing for interviewing sessions are:
■ knowing exactly what you want to ask: you need to have a brainstorm with pupils about what is already known and what they want to know
■ preparing good questions: explain about open and closed questions. Closed questions ask for a factual, limited type of answer. For example, asking 'How long have you been a planning officer?' or 'What do you do?' will give you the bare facts. Open questions give

more room for an opinion, and may reveal more about the person. For example, 'What do you like most and least about being a councillor?' or 'What do you feel is important about this area?' You will need a combination of both to make an interesting interview

■ being clear: questions should be unambiguous, and should follow a logical order, so that the interviewee is not forced to flit from topic to topic

■ making sure the physical conditions are right: decide if the whole class will be asking questions, or if the interview will be conducted by a smaller group. You need to check the location beforehand for comfort, space, and background noise. Knowing how to work the tape recorder is important, and details like ensuring that the batteries are charged, and the sound level is right, can make or break the session. Keeping the machine out of sight and the microphone as unobtrusive as possible helps towards a relaxed atmosphere.

Guidelines for the good interviewer include:

■ being friendly and addressing the person being interviewed by name. Many people are embarrassed, so it is up to you to put them at ease

■ being clear. Make sure you can be heard, and that the question is plainly understood

■ concentrating on what is being said. If you let your attention wander, the interviewee will also lose interest

■ being a good listener. Do not talk too much yourself

■ not interrupting. If they have gone off the point return to it by using a phrase like; 'Earlier on you were saying ...' or 'Can we go back to ...'

■ saying thank you when you have finished.

Pupils from Capenhurst Primary School interviewed staff at Chester Railway Station. They were evaluating what they liked and disliked about the station and produced large project booklets which were exhibited in the City Council Forum Offices.

WRITING AND RECORDING

LETTER WRITING

Letter writing skills are taught in school, but the exercise is more meaningful if the letter is written in a real situation. If the issue you are investigating is a live one, and if there has been interest in the local press, why not get your pupils to contribute to the debate by:

■ doing some research into what makes a good letter to a newspaper before pupils begin their own
■ collecting letters to the editor from a variety of local and regional newspapers over two or three weeks. Usually there is one issue that provokes a series of correspondence
■ cutting out these letters and use them to look at the use of language
■ working in small groups to use two different colours to highlight sentences which they consider to be fact (that can be checked and verified) and those which are opinion
■ sharing findings. Which letters are the most convincing? Which are the most persuasive? Which qualities does an editor look for in letters for publication?

USING JOURNALISTIC TECHNIQUES

A variety of journalistic techniques can be used as an approach for presenting the results of your pupils' investigations into a local issue. These offer various opportunities for developing skills in literacy alongside citizenship work.

Newspaper article

Your pupils might wish to write up their investigations in the form of a newspaper article. Your local newspaper might even print a series of articles, if your issue is of current interest to readers. Here are some helpful hints:

■ keep it short: 200-250 words is a good length for a newspaper story
■ make sure the first paragraph is exciting enough to attract the reader's attention, and to make them want to read on
■ use sub-headings to hold your reader's attention. Make sure these are relevant to your story
■ quotations from people involved in the story add interest. Make sure that these are accurate and credited
■ put important information at the beginning of your story. If the newspaper is short of space the editor may cut your story by removing paragraphs at the end.

Short bites of information

Written work does not always have to be presented in article format. Newspapers often present short pieces of information as bullet points. These have impact on the reader, and put the point across quickly and effectively. Writing in this format is not an easy skill. Get your pupils to practise by editing their own, or another's work and by summarising longer pieces of writing:

■ give your class a piece of printed text - a lengthy newspaper article or an extract from a history textbook
■ ask one group of pupils to summarise the information it contains into half the number of words, another into three-quarters the number, and another group to condense it into quarter the number of words. They may like to start by underlining or highlighting 'key sentences' in each paragraph
■ compare results between groups.

What has been left out? How has this altered the meaning of the piece? Have they written in note form or in full sentences? What effect does this have on the reader? Has summarising the text distorted the meaning of the original piece? Does the shortest piece have the most immediate impact?

■ your pupils can then apply this technique to their own findings about the issue they are investigating, and can present their information in short, lively bullet points.

RECORDING
Taking photographs

Photographs can be a valuable way to collect and record information whether in print, slide or digital form. If your pupils are going to produce a visual outcome such as a display, newspaper or website about a citizenship issue, then photographs can really make the publication come alive. Encourage your pupils to think about the photographs they are taking:

■ can the shot be taken from an unusual angle?
■ what about taking the photograph through an open doorway or up a staircase?

■ should you have people in your picture?

■ find an archive picture and take a shot today from the same vantage point. What has changed?

■ once you have taken your picture, should you crop or trim it to give it more impact?

■ limit the number of shots as this requires pupils to focus.

Video can be an exciting alternative to taking photographs. It is essential to plan the video using storyboards and to write scripts before filming starts.

Note taking

The skill of note taking cannot be left to chance. There are various techniques that can be used for collecting relevant and specific information during a site visit:

■ simple annotated sketching - as well as drawing or taking a photograph of your subject matter, ask your pupils to make some brief notes on specific aspects such as colour, materials or condition

■ observational note taking - to encourage limited observation, restrict pupils to only three observations about the subject

■ recording using a specially designed form

■ use a glossary of terms devised before the visit to annotate a picture of a building

■ use colour coding to annotate a plan or drawing

■ information can be classified into 'what we know' and 'what we need to find out'.

CASE STUDY

OUR HIGH STREET

Background

Upper Tean village has traditionally relied on the textile industry for employment. A linen mill had been making ribbons for use in a variety of products such as corsets, until it closed several years ago. Staffordshire Moorlands District Council successfully applied for a Heritage Economic Regeneration Scheme (HERS) grant from English Heritage to promote the repair and enhancement of the historic buildings in the conservation area within the village.

The project

Great Wood Primary School in Upper Tean, Staffordshire used a study of their local high street to involve all their pupils, including the Reception class, in thinking about citizenship and their local historic environment. Many linked the project to their existing local history or geography studies.
The Reception teacher used the High Street to:

■ to understand that it has a variety of buildings used for different purposes, for example homes and shops
■ to understand that different shops sell different products which are delivered and then sold
■ to look closely at some architectural features and understand the concept of old and new buildings.

What we did

Accompanied by three adults, the class walked along the High Street looking at the buildings and how they were used. They made drawings of what they saw and discussed which buildings they liked or disliked and why. The teacher explained why some shops were boarded up and the group talked about the traffic, its dangers and noise. Finally, they went inside a shop to look at what it sold.

The High Street was located within a conservation area and contained a number of listed buildings including the Mill.

Back in the classroom, the pupils' observations were reinforced through model-making. The model of the High Street was then used to discuss road safety and the green cross code through play. It was later displayed in the school hall as part of the end of term exhibition on the High Street. Parents, members of the village and guest experts were invited to view the displays.

Citizenship links
Pupils were taught:
■ to observe, problem solve and discuss (Early Learning Goal: exploration and investigation)
■ to find out about their environment and talk about its features (Early Learning Goal: sense of place)
■ to develop awareness of their own needs and views and be sensitive to the needs and views of others (Early Learning Goal: self-confidence and self-esteem).

➤ Conservation Areas pages 10-11, Listed Buildings pages 12-13
↘ Case Studies - Our High Street

What we had to say ...
Teacher: The teacher felt that making the model of the High Street was particularly successful as it was enjoyed by her pupils, it developed their design and making skills and reinforced what they had observed on their visit.

The model was displayed in the hall as part of the school's open week.

The children took turns to play with their model of the High Street using toy cars and play people.

CASE STUDY

REUSING OLD CHURCHES

Background

Churches become redundant when they are no longer needed as places of worship and like all redundant buildings, they can soon fall into disrepair. If the church is to be put to a new use and is architecturally significant it will need very careful conversion. In order to protect the original fabric, structures erected inside the building are usually self-supporting and any key features are retained. In Ipswich town centre there are seven redundant churches, one of which has already been converted for use as the Tourist Information Centre.

The project

Year 1 pupils at Eyke CECV Primary School in Suffolk used the issue of redundant churches as a focus for a cross-curricular approach to citizenship. The challenge was to think about ways that one of the redundant churches could be re-used in the future whilst still protecting the building.

What we did

The Year 1 teacher prepared for this project by talking to the local conservation officer and visiting two of the redundant churches - St Stephen's, that had been reused as a Tourist Information Centre, and the empty St Lawrence's. A scheme of work was written that linked the project to existing geography and RE studies. To introduce this project, the teacher built on prior work including a geography project looking at the school grounds and RE work on 'Special Places', when they had visited their local church and had looked at typical features. Pupils brainstormed the reasons why a church might become redundant.

On the day of the visit, pupils went first to St Stephen's. They worked in groups to look at the

Many redundant churches in the centre of towns are no longer in residential areas but now in the midst commercial businesses.

surviving features of the church and the temporary nature of new structures such as display shelves and counters. They also discussed the ambience of the building, in terms of their likes and dislikes.

Pupils then repeated this activity in St Lawrence's in order to make a comparison and were surprised by its dilapidated condition. They recorded materials, patterns, window design and features through sketching, and measured the length and width of the building. The teacher then introduced the idea of re-using the church in the same way that St Stephen's had been re-used and pupils brainstormed initial ideas on site. As well as surveying the interior of the church, pupils assessed the use of other buildings in the immediate locality.

Back at school pupils wrote sentences and drew pictures to show

their ideas. Six main themes emerged - dance hall, sports hall, swimming pool, fast food or ice cream parlour, hostel for the homeless, and a play area for children with a baby facility. Pupils were then spit into six groups, each taking a theme and brainstorming questions that they might wish to ask potential users.

Design boards and plans were created to show what would be included in their designs for the church.

What we had to say ...

Teacher: The teacher felt that the project had not only covered work in citizenship and design and technology, but also supported work in literacy and numeracy and encouraged pupils to work co-operatively in groups.

Pupils' models of the church of St Lawrence as a play centre.

Citizenship links

Pupils were taught:
■ to recognise likes and dislikes
■ to share opinions and explain views
■ to take part in discussions
■ to realise that people have needs
■ to identify what improves and harms their environment.

>Listed buildings pages 12-13, Buildings at Risk pages 14-15, Places of Worship pages 18-19
↘ Case Studies - Reusing old Churches, Temple Church

CASE STUDY

OUR HOME ZONE

Background

The concept of Home Zones seeks to make certain areas more family friendly by making the streets safer and less dominated by traffic. In Chester, the area between Francis Street and Egerton Street has been designated a pilot Home Zone as part of the Department of Transport's scheme to change the way that streets are used and to improve the quality of life in residential streets.

Egerton Street lies on the edge of the city centre and is dominated by a mix of traditional terrace housing and more recent high-density local authority flats and maisonettes, interspersed with small areas of open space. The Home Zone proposal hopes to create a sense of place/neighbourhood, improve accessibility for the most vulnerable of the community, and reclaim the streets for the residents by changing priorities and creating new open spaces and play areas, introducing traffic calming and rationalising parking.

The project

Children from Boughton St. Paul's Nursery and Infant School located in the Home Zone worked with Chester's SEEN (the Sustainable Environmental Education Network - see Contacts pages 68-69) to investigate the area round their school to determine what they liked about the area, and what they think could be improved to make the streets more attractive, more pedestrian friendly and less traffic dominated.

What we did

The school addressed two key areas for investigation:
- how did children play in the past? How do they play today at home and in the playground?
- how can the local area be improved so that everyone feels safer and more inclined to go out?

The children walked around the local area to set the context for their investigations. They were made more aware of how the past influences the present. For example, the houses built for the railway workers and for people working in industry sited by the canal were not built to cope with the volume of modern traffic.

The project began with a letter from the Head of Forward Planning for Chester City Council. He asked for the children's help in figuring out what they liked and did not like about their local area.

> Dear Children
> I know that you are finding out about your local area. I wonder if you will be able to help me? I am trying to find out what children like and don't like about the area near your school. I would also like to know what kind of things we could do to the area to make it a better place for children and families to live in. Can you think of any ways to in which we could make it a safer and better place for children to play out in?
> I look forward to seeing your ideas.
> Yours sincerely
> Head of Forward Planning
> Chester City Council

Back in school, the theme of play was explored in different ways through a series of activities:
■ a grandad was invited to talk about the local area in the past and how children played, allowing the children to view the historic environment through the eyes of someone who had lived there
■ old maps and photographs were studied to increase children's knowledge of the area and develop historical skills and concepts
■ as part of the Jubilee celebrations, the children were encouraged to take part in old-fashioned street games
■ a session at the Grosvenor Museum investigating the types of objects used in Victorian times, particularly for play.
The children visited Ellesmere Port Boat Museum to learn more about living by canals, similar to the children's own experience. The project culminated in ideas on play by designing and making clay tiles. These have been turned into a

triptych of three large pictures. After consultation with the community it is hoped to place this feature in the community, allowing the children to have a real effect on the development of a Home Zone culture in their area.

Citizenship links
Pupils were taught:
■ to share their opinions on things that matter to them and to explain their views
■ to realise that they belong to various groups and communities, such as family and school
■ to understand what improves and harms their local, natural and built environments and about some of the ways people look after them
■ to understand the rules for, and ways of keeping safe, including basic road safety, and about people who can help them to stay safe
■ to listen to other people, and play and work co-operatively
■ to take part in discussions
■ to meet and talk with people to consider social and moral dilemmas that they come across in everyday life.

> ➤ Contacts pages 68-69
> ↘ Case Studies - Our Home Zone, Our High Street, War Memorial

The principal engineer for Chester City Council came into school and talked to the children about his work and the Home Zone.

CASE STUDY   FAST FORWARD TO THE PAST

Background

Marsden and Slaithwaite in the Colne Valley near Huddersfield were undergoing major regeneration work including restoration work to seven miles of the Huddersfield Canal. The accompanying town regeneration work included Heritage Economic Regeneration Scheme (HERS) grants from English Heritage, for building repairs and environmental enhancement work in these conservation areas. This has led to the reopening of the canal and the development of a major tourist attraction, 'The Standedge Experience' at the end of the Colne Valley. Both towns have been used for filming popular television programmes and so the impact of tourists and the potential for benefits to the towns needed to be considered.

The project

Year 6 pupils from Marsden Junior School and Slaithwaite Junior and Infant School were tasked with producing a three-minute video that considered how the towns would be changing over the next ten years and whether the pupils could and would have any influence on the management of the historic environment in the future. The project also linked to their planned geography studies looking at the local environment.

What we did

The project involved pupils discussing what they liked about their town, what things they did not like and how they thought the regeneration work would affect it. They worked in small groups, discussing an aspect of their town they were concerned about, working out ideas and developing a storyboard and script for their video.

Each group visited their key filming points and made their three-minute videos. The pupils learnt to

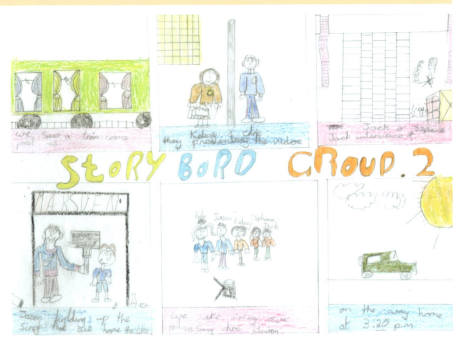

Pupils worked in groups to map their ideas. These were developed into storyboards with scripts.

A video project undertaken by Year 6 pupils of two primary schools in Marsden and Slaithwaite, which involved the children discussing what they did and did not like about the recent regeneration work taking place in their town.

use the large video cameras and tripods. The completed videos with displays of the pupils' work were shown to parents, school governors and the local planning officer, who then used the videos for discussions with local groups in the area.

The project was highly motivational for pupils who all worked well together, discussing and refining their ideas.

Citizenship links

Pupils were taught:

- to take part in discussions
- to recognise likes and dislikes
- to share opinions and explain views
- to identify what improves and harms their environment
- to understand that economic choices affect communities and the local environment
- to collaborate to produce a final product.

> Conservation Areas pages 10-11, Regeneration pages 24-25
Case Studies - Fast Forward to the Past, Our High Street

Filming on location

In addition to the video pupils presented their work to parents using display panels.

Pupils' designs for wastebins.

What we had to say ...

Pupil: "We were really pleased with how much we improved from when we first started rehearsing our video to when we actually did it. I think it came out quite well."

Pupil: "The brainstorming was easy because once we knew what we were doing ideas were flowing through our heads."

Teacher: "The finished videos were successful and present 'warts and all' but when it's considered that they were totally child-produced the pupils felt proud of their work and rightly so. It really gave the children a focus to the end of the term. They thoroughly enjoyed the project, even the hard bits, which we turned into positive learning experiences. The final presentation was very important for the children's esteem - to celebrate their hard work."

CASE STUDY | # BUILDING A BIO TOWN

Background

The Bio Town project was a cross curricular activity which aimed to include elements of citizenship, sustainability and environmental education as well as technology, geography, history and art.

The project

Year 6 pupils from Luckwell Primary School in South Bristol gained an understanding of archaeology and planning by creating a sustainable town in another country. It asked pupils to look at what essential things we need to live, including shelter.

What we did

The pupils visited Bristol to look at what makes up a living city, highlighting some of the problems including traffic and pollution. They also visited the Architecture Centre and took photographs of how buildings were being adapted. Back at school, a number of experts came in to participate in a question and answer session, and to offer a new challenge. An archaeologist told them that they may need to decide what to do about building their new town in an area where an amazing archaeological site of cultural importance had been found. The pupils were surprised at this new development because they had not previously considered this. The pupils discovered that the archaeologist had the right to stop the building.

The class then took on the roles of developers and archaeologists. They debated the issues surrounding this sudden find. What do we do? Move the town or stay and work around it? Give the archaeologists time to record the most important features and remove the finds? What do we do with the artefacts? A vote was taken to save some of the archaeology for visitors to see, excavate the rest and

The architectural designs of the new museum for the Bio Town reflected the archaeology and also the creative use of contemporary design.

build a new sustainable museum to exhibit the finds.

Models of the New Town were exhibited in the hall with a presentation at the school assembly. Other classes and parents were invited to view the models and exhibition.

Citizenship links

Pupils were taught:
■ to take part in discussions
■ to recognise likes and dislikes to share opinions and explain views
■ to identify what improves and harms their environment
■ to understand that economic choices affect communities and local environment
■ to learn about the range of jobs
■ to collaborate to produce a final product.

> ➤Archaeological Sites pages 8-9
> ⤢Case Studies - Building a Bio Town, Groundwell Ridge

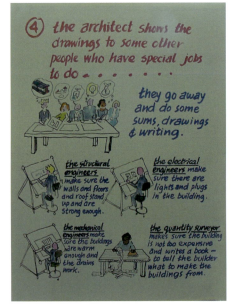

CASE STUDY

OUR PAST BELOW GROUND

Background

Segedunum and Arbeia are two of the Roman forts along Hadrian's Wall World Heritage Site. Both feature full scale reconstructions of Roman military buildings. Arbeia also has an interactive archaeological exhibition and Segedunum has a spectacular viewing tower giving a panoramic view of the site and an extensive interactive exhibition. In contrast, Chesters Roman Fort has a less developed approach to interpreting the site for visitors.

Part of the multi-media interactive exhibition.

One of the reconstructed buildings at Arbeia.

The museum at Chesters.

Assessing the visitor experience.

The project

The project took place over three days with year seven pupils, who were given three tasks:

■ investigate, compare and evaluate the ways in which the past is presented to the public at Segedunum and Arbeia

■ explore the site at Chesters and suggest ways that it could be improved for visitors

■ work in teams to prepare a proposal recommending improvements to Chesters.

What we did

After being given the brief, and learning how to use the digital video cameras and the accompanying software, pupils visited Arbeia, Segedunum and Chesters. Working in teams, they evaluated each site in terms of their appeal to the public and how they were interpreted for different groups of visitors, considering elements such as signage, interactive exhibits and reconstructions. They took notes and recorded pertinent features using still images and video. Pupils also considered access issues for different types of visitor, particularly children, the elderly and disabled people.

On the final day, each team collated their evidence and discussed the limitations of development at Chesters owing to environmental and archaeological factors. Then they formulated ideas for improving the site, which were presented using PowerPoint. Pupils had four hours to complete this task. Afterwards, families were invited to watch the presentations along with a judging panel consisting of representatives from the three sites. Each team had five minutes to sell their ideas to the panel, and proposed some excellent solutions for overcoming environmental restrictions at Chesters. One team suggested that tree houses might accommodate hidden viewing platforms with interactive exhibits, while installing ground level screens to assist disabled visitors.

Citizenship links

Pupils were taught:

■ to respect and value the environment, and that they have some responsibility for it

■ to express rational arguments having researched social, moral and environmental issues

■ to present opinions, values and beliefs confidently, clearly and concisely

■ to consider the needs of different groups of visitors

■ to negotiate and contribute to making decisions as part of a responsible group.

> Archaeological Sites pages 8-9
⬄ Berkhamsted Castle, Portchester Castle, Our past below ground

CASE STUDY   FUTURETOWN AND BEYOND

Background

Over the past twenty years or so, Gravesend in Kent, has seen a decline in its traditional commercial and economic base, which had been primarily focused on the town's role as a river port and associated industries. Gravesend is in an area of the South East close to two of the largest out of town shopping developments in Britain. Experience across the country has shown that proximity to large out of town retail centres can spell disaster for traditional town centre shopping streets. Gravesham Borough Council took co-ordinated action early on to work within wider regional and county initiatives, to maintain and develop Gravesend's position as a place where people want to live, are able to work and do business, and which attracts visitors to a variety of leisure activities and shopping. A priority was the repair and re-use of many of the town's historic buildings, which provide a link between Gravesend's past, present and future. A decision was taken to involve young people and community groups in particular, as citizens of the town, and several educational programmes have been given support and a high profile by the Council.

The project

'Futuretown' is a national scheme to raise awareness among young people of the importance of our towns and cities. In Gravesend, 'Futuretown and Beyond' (FAB) takes this a step further by involving over twenty schools and community groups, higher education institutions, the local authority and commercial organisations in a three year project. This project uses creativity and ICT to create a model of how citizens can contribute to and promote potential 'futures' for theirtown centre. It is

Milton Place was originally a prosperous residential area of Gravesend, but by the 1990s it was run down and had been inappropriately 'modernised'. These large houses have now been restored and provide town centre accommodation for several families.

centred round creating a 'global town square' - a place of debate and interaction for all.

What we did

Young people from a local school were taken off their normal timetable for a week, to work exclusively on the FAB project.

They were given the brief of identifying an area where additional activity or facility was needed to make an improvement to the town. They had to set up and carry out their own research into what was lacking, put together their own proposals and present them to Gravesham Borough Council. At

The Town Pier was originally a hive of activity in the nineteenth and early twentieth centuries. With the decline in shipping trade since the Second World War, the pier deteriorated, and was identified as a 'Building at Risk'. This pier has been recently restored by Gravesham Borough Council, and will provide a riverside focus for both visitors and local residents.

Northfleet School for Girls presented their ideas for the future of Gravesend in a slide show which they sent to a school in Japan.

FAB Website homepage.

all stages of the process the pupils were asked to evaluate their own work, and how well they had managed to negotiate with the rest of their group. The Council is taking on board several of their proposals and ideas.

Workshops exploring the themes of 'You-topias' and 'Futures' - looking at themselves and their surroundings as they are in the here and now - provided material which has been put onto the town website as well as a dedicated FAB site. These images are exhibited at TOWNCENTRIC (the Tourism, Regeneration and Information Centre) and projected onto a six-metre 'Mega-screen' in the town centre. Gravesham Borough Council (with the support of other partners) is saying that wherever possible and practical, it will incorporate these ideas into its future plans for the town's development. Shoppers, children and those waiting for buses in the centre of Gravesend can now watch animat-

ed displays of work produced by schools, communicating their ideas about the future of their town and neighbourhoods.

Selection of 'You-topias' electronic postcards that can be viewed on the futuretown website.

Citizenship links

Pupils were taught:
- to respect and value the environment
- to believe that they have some responsibility for the environment
- to express rational arguments having researched social, moral and environmental issues
- to present opinions, values and

beliefs confidently, clearly and concisely
- to empathise with others and express opinions that are not necessarily their own
- to negotiate and contribute to making decisions as part of a responsible group
- to apply personal strengths to group tasks
- to understand the processes involved in working together.

> Buildings At Risk pages 14-15, Regeneration pages 24-25
> Futuretown and Beyond, Dover, Change in Ouseburn.

Proposals for re-designing the Clock Tower by Gravesend Grammar School for Boys.

CASE STUDY   CHANGE IN OUSEBURN

Background

The Ouseburn Valley lies just outside the city centre of Newcastle upon Tyne, with a striking and unusual townscape combining heritage, riverside and open space, running down to the River Tyne and the city's historic Quayside.

A base for the manufacture of lead, iron, soap, lime and pottery in the eighteenth and nineteenth centuries, the Valley declined in the twentieth century as industries closed. However, after decades of neglect, the area is now experiencing redevelopment and is home to a wide variety of businesses, many of them based in renovated buildings.

There are also many community and charitable organisations in the Valley which actively contribute to the character and vitality of the area.

The project

The project was part of a summer school programme for gifted and talented pupils, during which they looked at life in Ouseburn in the recent and distant past. They investigated the area in groups, meeting with individuals and organisations active in the valley. They then adopted causes in support of a range of interest groups concerned about the impact that new residents and businesses with different values and priorities might have on existing activities.

What we did

First, there was a presentation about the history of the area using sources from the local studies library. Then pupils visited Ouseburn to find out what is left and why so many people want to protect the area. Afterwards they met with residents to consider aspects of the area's recent history and listen to their concerns about the ongoing redevelopment work.

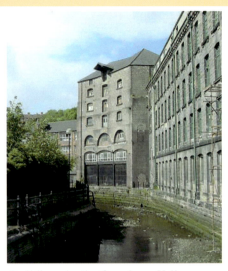
Buildings in the Ouseburn Valley.

Meeting residents of the Ouseburn and finding out about their lives and interests.

Discussing local issues in St Ann's Church.

Interviewing staff who work at the stables.

Pupils used tape recordings, photographs and notes to record their findings.

Visiting in groups they went to St Ann's Church to meet the vicar and a representative from the Friends of St Ann's. This beautiful eighteenth-century church has close associations with both the Ouseburn and the Quayside. The redevelopment of the Quayside has swept away St Ann's traditional working class parishioners and replaced them with higher income apartment owners and office-based professionals. Pupils heard how this change presents both opportunities and threats to St Ann's, and how the Friends of St Ann's were reaching out to the newcomers whilst protecting the cultural heritage and values of the past.

At Stepney Bank Stables, run as a charity, volunteers introduced the students to a riding project that helps children and young adults acquire self confidence and life skills. Here, they were given a tour of the charity's historic Victorian premises, built for a parcel express company in the days of horse drawn road haulage - providing a shining example of how imaginative new uses can be made of buildings which might otherwise be demolished.

Then pupils visited one of the Valley's pigeon lofts to meet the Secretary of the local Homing Association. Pigeon racing was once one of the most popular pastimes, but is now declining rapidly. Pupils were fascinated by their host's account of this traditional sport and most of them eagerly took up the chance to handle a racing pigeon.

There were also visits to the Victoria Tunnel, built in 1839-41 to carry coal to the Tyne from a mine in the centre of the city. Keen volunteer guides now take

Exploring the area's industrial heritage.

Designing and producing newsletters.

interested people into the Tunnel to see how it was constructed and then converted in 1939 to serve as an air raid shelter.

Back at their base, students discussed their visit, their thoughts and observations of the area and the people who lived and worked in it, and shared concerns over the future of the Valley. Working in

Remains of the Valley's industrial past.

pairs they took up particular causes and used desk top publishing programmes to create newsletters and campaign leaflets to highlight key issues, using digital photographs and written notes taken during their visit.

The newsletters reflected the pupils' understanding of the value of the area and the individual buildings within it, as well as giving an insight into the attitudes of local people and their traditions.

Citizenship links

Pupils were taught:
■ how people lived in a past industrial community and how different their lives were to ours
■ how communities need a variety of buildings with varying functions in order to survive

■ how and why areas change and how this affects people living and working within it
■ to appreciate how economic choices affect communities and the local environment
■ to identify what makes an area special and why people may want to preserve its character
■ to respect the opinions and beliefs of others and campaign on their behalf about the voluntary work of individuals and groups who worked to preserve their locality and traditions.

> Archaeological Sites pages 8-9
↘ Our Past Below Ground, Berkhamsted Castle, Portchester Castle, Change in Ouseburn

CHURCH FIGHTS NEW BUILDINGS

St. Ann's church in the east of Newcastle is trying to make it in the 21st century. Reverend Chris Savage is trying to bring the community back to the church. There are regular Concerts and activities. So far he has been very successful in doing so. The most recent is this Sunday the Vintage Jazzmen that starts at 7pm till 9pm. His parish St. Ann's is in jeopardy thanks to the million pound projects that are going on at the moment at the Quayside. The church will soon be Obstructed from view from over the river as the new luxury apartments and offices are erected. It is a rigorous task for the parish to keep it alive but one the reverend says will be worth while.

THE DAILY HERALD

INSIDE... OUSEBURN REVIVED!

The Stepney Stables in the west end of Newcastle. Has been an independent charity for 5 years.

this mean's that the stables owners cannot make any profit or gain from this service. The stables contains 14 horses and ponies and is expecting another arrival in the near future.

The Stables can only survive with the funding from companies and donations from the public. Last year the stable workers nearly had to cut their wages by 50% because of the lack of funds. The Stables help children who have learning difficulties and autistic problems. Horses riding is considered by many experts to be very good treatment for cerebral palsy. The horses need feeding a lot, The horses feed and hay, cost approximately £900 per month. Plus the horses need their hooves re-shoed every 6 weeks with a cost of £35 per hove.

YELL.COM

The Evening Chronicle

Wednesday 24th July 2002 — Newcastle Edition — 35p

Community spirit

Community Spirit has officially hit the east end of Newcastle. Along the Ouseburn, a tributary of the River Tyne, community spirit is on a all time high. Several community projects have brought the people of the area together.

Stepney Bank Stables is one of these. First used as a holding area for animals to be slaughtered. The stables are now a nonprofit charity, and although they charge £5 for riding lessons, the money made is spent on the needs of the horses for example veterinary care, feed, bedding, shoeing. The animals have comfortable stables compared to when it was a haulage company when they only had small stalls. Many different types of people from the surrounding community use the facilities, such as people with special needs, disabilities and emotional problems. They are brought together by their love of horses.

St. Ann's Church has strong community links. It was originally built in 1768, it was dark, cold, and very old fashioned until it was redeveloped because of structural problems in the 60-70's. Like most of the coun-

try mainly older people attend the church, the vicar Chris Savage said 'I would like more people to attend although it is not the done thing these days'.

St Ann's Church has benefited from a Heritage Lottery funded community education project. The overall aim of the project is to develop St Ann's as a venue for children to discover the history, geography and habitat of the area. Historically, the church is the centre of the community, providing facilities for all ages. Although the sight of the church will be blocked from the Tyne by the development of apartments further down the bank.

Continued on page 2.

Metro Centre

Page 1

CASE STUDY THE WHITEFRIARS PROJECT

Background

The historic centre of Canterbury, with its cathedral and medieval buildings, attracts visitors from all over the world. In 1942, one night of bombing almost completely destroyed the southern end of the city's main street. In the 1950s and 1960s this part of the city was rebuilt. The area known as Whitefriars, after the medieval friary which once occupied the site, is being redeveloped again to improve facilities in Canterbury.

The project

St. Nicholas School in Canterbury provides education for young people aged between 4 and 19 who have severe learning difficulties. All the pupils from classes 3, 4 and Senior 1 (Key Stages 2 and 3) took part in the project.
 The project covered a wide range of curriculum areas as well as citizenship, which concentrated on developing the pupils' knowledge and understanding of the local environment - how the local area has changed over a long period of time, how it might change in the future, and how people can improve the environment through detailed planning.

What we did

The pupils were given the opportunity to experience the sights, sounds and smells of Canterbury and the Whitefriars site. They were asked to look at and identify the equipment being used around the site and take photographs using a digital camera. They also recorded the sounds around them using video and audio tape recorders. The children experienced first-hand that buildings were being demolished and new buildings emerging. In a later visit they went to watch the archaeologists at work, at an exhibition area called 'The Big Dig'.

St. Nicholas' School exhibited their work, alomg with many other schools, at the Canterbury Environment Centre. (Photograph shows pupils and parents from other schools).

The pupils also spent some time in the old St. Andrew's Church. They took photographs and made observational sketches. Prior to the visit they thought of questions they would like to ask about the church during their visit. The children were given the opportunity to ask these questions and were encouraged to record the answers. A second visit was made to introduce the idea that the building would be re-built on a new site. This was followed up by visits to watch the new church being built. Photographs were taken as evidence of the changes that had been made.
 For pupils with profound and multiple learning difficulties, sensory cues were used throughout to gain attention, aid memory and establish atmosphere. Sound clues were used to help pupils understand the key features. Therefore, a major part of the project was to create a sensory story about the Whitefriars site and their own thoughts about its future redevel-

opment. This was developed into a 'Big Book', which included drawings, photographs and writing with symbols. A drama piece related to the story involved interaction and participation with all members of the group.

Citizenship links

Pupils were taught:
■ to develop confidence and responsibility, making the most of their abilities
■ to prepare to play an active role as citizens
■ to research, discuss and debate topical issues, problems and events
■ to develop good relationships and respect the differences between people
■ to think about the lives of people living in other places and times, and people with different values and customs.

➤Regeneration pages 24-25
↙Whitefriars, The Old Orphanage, Portchester Castle

THE OLD ORPHANAGE

Background

The 'Union Orphanage' is a Grade 2 listed building in the East End of Sunderland. Built in 1861 as an orphanage for mariners' children, it has had a chequered history of occupation after its closure in 1939. It was used as a base for the Home Guard during the Second World War and then as a community centre, which was recently, relocated to newer premises nearby.

The project

This was an extension of a local study in history by a group of students with special learning needs who were looking into the development of the port of Sunderland. The project had a strong art approach where students communicated their findings visually.

What we did

On their first visit, students took drawings and photographs of the building, focusing on its design, the materials used and interesting architectural features, such as decoration, window surrounds, chimneys and gates. They also used words and short phrases to record their feelings about the atmosphere of the building and its surroundings.

On their return to school, students researched the social history

Recording significant features.

of the building using material provided by the local studies library. To help their research, they composed a letter to the local newspaper asking for information from readers who had connections with the building either as an orphanage or as a base for the Home Guard. They also visited the local community centre to talk to the residents and see a photographic display.

Following the appeal for information, a number of former residents contacted the school. Some agreed to be interviewed by students, who conducted short taped interviews.

The group agreed that the building was important and decided that something should be done to highlight this to the local community and to the City of Sunderland to gain support for its future survival. Owing to the special

needs of the students, the teacher suggested that this could be effectively achieved in a visual way - a textile hanging that could be suspended inside one of the boarded-up windows, which would portray aspects of the building's past.

Putting the banner in place.

Citizenship links

Pupils were taught:
■ to work together to make decisions, based on informed opinions, that the rest of the group adopt
■ to collaborate on joint activities
■ to invite external people to contribute towards their project and make arrangements for them to visit the school, which also introduce them to the world of work
■ to consider the reasons for preserving old buildings
■ how legislation controls the way that buildings and our environment are protected or developed (political literacy)

Agreeing on the content of the banner.

CONTACTS

Ancient Monuments Society
Study the conservation of ancient monuments and historic buildings of all ages.
St Ann's Vesty Hall, 2 Church Entry, London EC4V 5HB
Tel: 0207 236 3934
www.ancientmonumentssociety.org.uk

Archaeological Units
Archaeological units will have information about sites and finds. An archaeologist may be able to come into school to talk to your class. There may be an excavation in progress that you can go to see. Ring your local council to ask for a contact. Also contact the Education Officer at the Council for British Archaeology, Bowes Morrell House, 111 Walmgate, York YO1 9WA Tel: 01904 671417
www.britarch.ac.uk

Archives
Archive centres will be able to help with historic documents. Not all areas have their own archives department, and you may have to contact your County Record Office or search the national list of archives at
www.hmc.gov.uk/archon

Association of Industrial Archaeology
An organisation that promotes industrial archaeology.
www.industrial-archaeology.org.uk

CABE
The Commission for Architecture and the Built Environment (CABE) aims to ensure through its Education foundation greater public understanding of the importance of quality urban design and stimulate learning about and through the built environment. Ultimately it aims to help develop more informed, confident and demanding citizens. Free to join network including regular 360∞ magazine.
CABE Education, The Tower Building, 11 York Road, London SE1 7NX Tel: 020 7960 2400
www.cabe.org.uk

Churches Conservation Trust
Cares for over 300 churches of historical, architectural or archaeological importance, but no longer needed for regular worship. Educational support includes free visits, teacher's booklets on over 40 sites and introductory sessions for teachers. Contact the Education Officer.
1 West Smithfield, London EC1A 9EE Tel: 020 7213 0679
www.visitchurches.org.uk

Civic Trust
This is the name given to an umbrella organisation for local amenity societies from all around the country. The Civic Trust campaigns for local building and environmental issues, and will be a good source of information and local knowledge about the area and planning issues. It also organises the popular annual Heritage Open Days event each year in association with English Heritage. Ask at your local library, or apply to the national headquarters for general information.
17 Carlton House Terrace, London SW17 5AW
Tel: 020 7930 0914
www.civictrust.org.uk

Council for the Protection of Rural England (CPRE)
Warwick House, 25 Buckingham Palace Road, London SW1W 0PP
Tel: 020 7976 6433
www.cpre.org.uk

English Heritage
This is the government's principal advisor on the historic environment, with responsibility for its protection and promoting public understanding and support. It works with local authorities, owners, developers, regional agencies and others to ensure that change is managed positively for the benefit of future generations and to strengthen local economies. For comprehensive information on its work including Buildings at Risk, listed buildings and support materials for teachers, see the website.
www.english-heritage.org.uk
(see also NMR)

Garden History Society
Promotes study, protection and conservation of historic parks and gardens.
77 Cowcross Street, London EC1M 6BP Tel: 020 7608 2409
www.gardenhistorysociety.org.uk

Georgian Group
Promotes appreciation of
Georgian heritage.
6 Fitzroy Square, London W1P
6DX Tel: 020 7387 1720
www.georgiangroup.org.uk

Learning through Landscapes
Learning through Landscapes is
the National School Grounds
Charity. They work with schools
and organisations across the
country to help them improve and
develop their school grounds.
www.ltl.org.uk

Local Studies Library
Local studies libraries will help
you find documentary sources
such as maps and census records.
They will probably also know of
local contacts such as history societies. Look in your telephone
directory for a contact address.

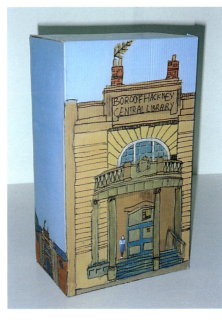

Museums
Your local museum may have an
education officer or curator who
can provide you with information
and possibly lend you items from
their collection.

**National Monuments Record
(NMR)**
English Heritage's public archive
of over 10 million items can be a
useful starting point for information on the historic environment.

www.pastscape.org
Images of England (photographs
and descriptions of listed buildings
and structures in England)
www.imagesofengland.org.uk

The Newspaper Society
Bloomsbury House, 74-77 Great
Russell Street, London WC1 3DA
Tel: 020 7636 7014

Planning Authority
Your local planning department
will have information on the past
and present development plans for
the area, and can explain planning
procedures. It might be possible to
get photocopies of maps, or other
relevant information, like past
development plans. Ask if a plan-
ner is able to meet your class,
either at school or in the planning
offices, to talk to about the
process. Do bear in mind that,
with their normal workload, it may
not always be feasible.

Public Record Office
Kew, Richmond, Surrey
TW9 4DU Tel: 020 8876 3444
www.pro.gov.uk

**Royal Institute of British
Architects (RIBA)**
66 Portland Place, London
W1N 4AD Tel: 020 7580 5533
www.riba.org

SAVE Britain's Heritage
Campaigns to save endangered
historic buildings.
68 Battersea High Street, London
SW11 3HX Tel: 020 7228 3336
www.savebritainsheritage.org.uk

SEEN
SEEN is the Sustainable
Environmental Education
Network. It is a partnership
between Chester City Council,
Cheshire County Council, the
Cheshire Society of Architects and
the Royal Society for the Arts. It
involves local children in real
design, planning and regeneration
issues from their community. It

gives children and young people a
voice, encouraging them to feed in
their views and is thus an important part of community consultation.
www.chestercc.gov.uk/heritage/
education/seen1.html

**Sites and Monuments Record
(SMR)**
Most SMRs are now held on a
computer database, but methods
of public access vary from area to
area. Some SMRs are accessible
directly through the Internet, for
example Durham SMR
(www.durham.gov.uk). In other
cases contact the Sites and
Monuments Officer either with an
enquiry or to book a time to visit
the SMR office.

**Society for the Protection of
Ancient Buildings (SPAB)**
37 Spital Square, London E1 6DY
Tel: 020 7377 1644
www.spab.org.uk

Twentieth Century Society
Promotes appreciation of
twentieth-century buildings.
70 Cowcross Street, London
EC1M 6BP Tel: 020 7412 7353
www.c20society.demon.co.uk

Victorian Society
Campaigns to save Victorian and
Edwardian buildings.
1 Priory Gardens, London
W4 1TT
www.victorian-society.org.uk

FURTHER READING AND INFORMATION

Publications

Allen, S, Hollinshead, L, & Wilkinson, S, **Using Houses and Homes**, English Heritage, 1998 ISBN 1-85074-398-3

Anderson, C, Planel, P, & Stone, P, **Stonehenge, a teacher's handbook**, English Heritage, 1995 ISBN 1-85074-312-6

Barnicoat, J,

Newspapers & Conservation, English Heritage, 1994 ISBN 1-85074-511-0

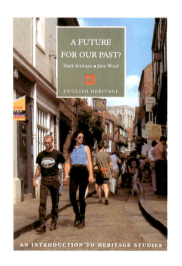

Brisbane, M, & Wood, J, **A Future For Our Past?**, English Heritage, 1996 ISBN 1-85074-491-2

Corbishley, M, **Aerial Photography**, English Heritage, 2004 ISBN 1-85074-780-6

Corbishley, M, Darvill, T, & Stone, P, **Prehistory**, English Heritage, 2000 ISBN 1-85074-325-8

Corbishley, M (ed.), **Primary History**, English Heritage, 1999 ISBN 1-85074-650-8

David, R, **History At Home**, English Heritage, 1996 ISBN 1-85074-591-9

Davies, I, & Webb, C, **Using Documents**, English Heritage, 1996 ISBN 1-85074-492-0

Keen, J, **Ancient Technology**, English Heritage, 1996 ISBN 1-85074-448-3

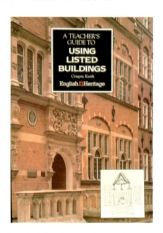

Keith, C, **Using Listed Building**s, English Heritage, 1991 ISBN 1-85074-297-9

Marcus, S, & Barker, R, **Using Historic Parks and Gardens**, English Heritage, 1997 ISBN 1-85074-510-2

Morris, R, & Corbishley, M, **Churches, Cathedrals and Chapels**, English Heritage, 1996 ISBN 1-85074-447-5

Planel, P, **Battlefields, Defence, Conflict and Warfare**, English Heritage, 1995 ISBN 1-85074-590-0

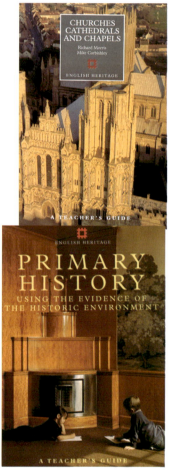

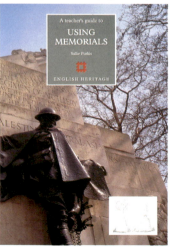

Purkis, S, **Using Memorials**, English Heritage, 1995 ISBN 1-85074-493-9

Purkis, S, **Using School Buildings**, English Heritage, 1993 ISBN 1-85074-379-7
Walmsley, D, **Hadrian's Wall**, a teacher's handbook, English Heritage, 2002 ISBN 1-85074-823-3
Wheatley, G, **World Heritage Sites**, English Heritage, 1997 ISBN 1-85074-446-7

Posters
English Parish Church, The Open Churches Trust, 1995
Hadrian's Wall Poster Pack, English Heritage, 2003 ISBN 1-85074-811-X
Time Detectives Poster Games, English Heritage, 2001 ISBN 1-85074-778-4

Photopacks
Britain Since 1930, National Monuments Record, English Heritage, 1998 ISBN 873592-44-2
Seaside Holidays in the Past, National Monuments Record, English Heritage, 2001 ISBN 873592-51-5
Victorians At Work, National Monuments Record, English Heritage, 1999 ISBN 873592-43-4
Victorian Transport, National Monuments Record, English Heritage, 1999 ISBN 873592-46-9

Videos
Our Past, Our Future, English Heritage, 2004. Will help teachers to deliver citizenship studies including KS2 Unit 9 Respect for Property and help pupils to understand the issues involved in protecting the historic built environment.

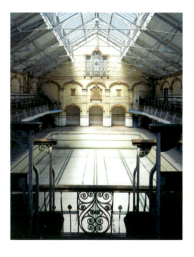

Getting in the Swim - exploring Manchester's 'water palace', English Heritage, 2002. Follows a Y5 project based on the Victoria Baths. Available on free loan. Tel 01761 452966.

Web links
Web links are also listed for many of the organisations on pages 68-69.

Built Environment
UNESCO www.unesco.org
United Kingdom Association of Building Preservation Trusts (APT) www.heritage.co.uk/apt

Buildings Book Trust, Yale University Press www.lookingatbuildings.org.uk

Archives
Commonwealth War Graves Commission www.cwgc.org.uk
National Register of Archive Repositories (maintained by the Historic Manuscripts Commission) www.hmc.gov.uk/archon/archon.htm
Public Record Office www.pro.gov.uk
Society of Archivists in Education Group (advice an accessing archive sources) www.archives.org.uk/education

Maps
Getmapping www.getmapping.com
Old maps www.old-maps.co.uk
Ordnance Survey www.ordsvy.gov.uk
Streetmap (commercial modern map information) www.Streetmap.co.uk
Up My Street www.upmystreet.com
Wildgoose www.wgoose.co.uk

Local History
British Association for Local History www.balh.co.uk/education.htm

Resources
The British Newspaper Library www.bl.uk
The Newspaper Society www.newspapersoc.org.uk

Case Studies
Gravesend www.futureandbeyond.co.uk
www.towncentric.co.uk
Home Zone, Chester www.homezones.org.uk
Victoria Baths, Manchester www.victoriabaths.org.uk

Urban archaeological databases
English Heritage is supporting a national programme of surveys of the archaeology, topography and historic buildings of England's historic towns and cities. The results will help local authorities, English Heritage and others to care for the fabric of our towns and cities in the future.
The database sources include archaeological excavations and other discoveries; information about historic buildings; historic maps; historic documents; and published literature. There will also be a summary report on the history, archaeology and historic topography of the town in question.

ACKNOWLEDGEMENTS AND CREDITS

Acknowledgements
English Heritage Education would like to thank all the pupils, staff, parents and community members from all the schools that have contributed to this book and CD-ROM.

Berkhamstead Castle
Hilary Catchpole, The Thomas Coram C of E Middle School
Patricia Ford, Hertfordshire Education Business Partnership;

Bio Town
Julia Christmas, Luckwell Primary School, Bristol;

Customs House
Anne Curtis
TEDCO (Tyneside Economic Development Company)
Staff of the English Department at Hebburn Comprehensive School;

Fast Forward
Staff and pupils at Marsden Junior School and Slaithwaite Junior & Infant School
Navdeep Kandola;

Futuretown and Beyond
Gravesham Borough Council and local Schools;

Groundwell Ridge
Nickey Pardoe, Swindon Borough Council;

Ipswich Redundant Churches
Staff and pupils of Eyke CEVC Primary School, Suffolk
Bob Kindred, Conservation Officer, Ipswich Borough Council
Linda Cartwright, Teacher Placement Manager, Suffolk Education Business Partnership
Ipswich Historic Churches Trust;

Liverpool Ropewalks
Staff and pupils of St Andrews CE Primary School, Maghull, Merseyside;

Oswestry Railway Station
Staff and pupils from The Marches School, Oswestry
Oswestry Borough Council
Shropshire Records and Research;

Our High Street, Upper Tean
Gill Bayliss, Conservation Officer, Staffordshire Moorlands District Council
Annette Davies and Joan Bennett, Staffordshire QLS
Michael Taylor, Historic Areas Adviser, English Heritage;

Ouseburn
Liz Cowans, Sacred Heart School, Fenham, Newcastle upon Tyne Excellence in Cities Programme; Mike Greatbatch and Alison Stancliffe, Ouseburn Heritage Education Programme;

Our Past Below Ground
Claire Johnson, Inspector for Gifted & Talented Provision, North Tyneside LEA and Excellence in Cities Partnership
University of Manchester Field Archaeology Centre;

Streets Ahead
Streets Ahead was run by Junction Arts, a community arts organisation, in partnership with English Heritage;

The Old Orphanage
Sue Harrow, Felstead School
Residents of East End, Sunderland
Staff of East End Community Centre, Sunderland;

The Old Fire Station
Staff of Redby Primary School
Sid Ord and Dennis Barker, former fire fighters;

Victoria Baths, Manchester
Trustees of the Victoria Baths Trust
Staff and pupils of Plymouth Road Primary School, Manchester;

War memorials - Remembrance Day
Margaret Read, Forsbrook Primary School and Christine Wardle, May Bank Infants, Staffordshire
Joan Bennett, Staffordshire QLS;

Water Tower gardens, Home Zone, Chester Railway Station
Chester's SEEN
Mike Hardman, Stephanie Higgins, Pauline Sharp from Chester City Council;

Whitefriars, Canterbury
Staff and pupils from St Peter's Methodist Primary School, St Stephen's Primary School, St Thomas' RC School, Payne Smith CE Primary School and St Nicholas School
Jo Gunne;

Whitehaven
Rob David & Cliff O'Neill, St Martin's College, Lancaster
Steve Milledge, Cockermouth School
Gareth Johnstone, Central Lancaster High School;

Credits
All photographs and drawings are the copyright of English Heritage except for Gravesham Borough Council 1, 62, 63; Frank Driessen 5br, 11 (all except map); Chester City Council 7(all), 23 (all), 37br, 48-49 (all), 56-57 (all); Newsquest Wiltshire/Evening Advertiser 9ml; Tony Bartholomew 10t, Peter Anderson 10m; John Stonard 11tl; John Yates tm; Barbara Evripidou Bristol Evening Post 19; Forsbrook Primary School 21 (all); Sandy Roy 24 (all); Brian Sherwen Copeland Borough Council 25t; Somerset Record Office 27t, English Heritage.NMR 26t, 27mr, 29t, 30 (all), 38bl; Public Record Office 27bl; Wolverhampton Archives & Local Studies 28br & bl; Ordnance Survey 29b; Crown Copyright.NMR 31br & bl; Chris Welch 32-33 (all except Oxford Mail and Times); David Walmsley 34-35 (all); Gravesham Borough Council 38, 62-63 (all); Great Wood Primary School 52-5 (all); Liz Cowans 64-65 (all); David Walmsley, Building Exploratory Hackney 68-69 (all).

English Heritage Education
We aim to help teachers at all levels to use the resource of the historic environment. Each year, we welcome half a million pupils, students and teachers on free educational group visits to over 400 historic sites in our case. We also offer services to help access the National Monument Record, our public archive. For free copies of our Free Educational Visits booklet, our Resources catalogue, and *Heritage Learning*, our termly magazine, contact:

English Heritage Education
Freepost 22 (WD214)
London
W1E 7EZ
Tel 0870 333 1181
E-mail:
education@english-heritage.org.uk
www.english-heritage.org.uk/education